RAND NATIONAL DEFENSE RESEARCH INSTITUTE

T0108952

Monitoring Social Media

Lessons for Future Department of Defense
Social Media Analysis in Support of
Information Operations

William Marcellino, Meagan L. Smith, Christopher Paul,
Lauren Skrabala

Prepared for the Office of the Secretary of Defense

For more information on this publication, visit www.rand.org/t/RR1742

Library of Congress Cataloging-in-Publication Data is available for this publication.
ISBN: 978-0-8330-9820-7

Published by the RAND Corporation, Santa Monica, Calif.
© Copyright 2017 RAND Corporation
RAND® is a registered trademark.

Cover: sdecoret/Fotolia.

Support RAND
Make a tax-deductible charitable contribution at
www.rand.org/giving/contribute

www.rand.org

Preface

Social media is playing an important and increasing role in U.S. military information operations (IO), because people around world, including civilian populations, U.S. allies, and U.S. adversaries, use social media platforms to share information and persuade others. The rapid growth of the communication technologies that underpin social media platforms has given nonstate adversaries an asymmetric advantage, as have the low cost of entry and the relative operational agility with which they, in contrast to established bureaucracies, can access and utilize new technologies. And so, while there are compelling national security reasons to field a social media analysis capability, the U.S. Department of Defense (DoD) must do so both while navigating U.S. law and cultural norms and under conditions of great uncertainty. Amid quickly evolving technologies and communication trends, there is a risk that DoD could invest in soon-to-be obsolete capabilities or encounter other challenges in building its analytic capacity and applying it in an effective and practical manner.

This report explores these complex issues and offers DoD a set of recommendations for building a social media analysis capability in support of IO that ably and appropriately enhances national security. It should be of particular interest to the U.S. military joint information operations community. Given both the urgency and the challenges in developing this capacity, and in light of a congressionally mandated assessment, DoD has a clear need for a research survey of the existing literature on social media analysis technologies, best practices, legal and ethical constraints to social media analysis, and the intersection of IO and social media analytics.

This research was sponsored by the Combating Terrorism Technical Support Office and conducted within the International Security and Defense Policy Center of the RAND National Defense Research Institute, a federally funded research and development center sponsored by the Office of the Secretary of Defense, the Joint Staff, the Unified Combatant Commands, the Navy, the Marine Corps, the defense agencies, and the defense Intelligence Community.

For more information on the RAND International Security and Defense Policy Center, see www.rand.org/nsrd/ndri/centers/isdp or contact the director (contact information is provided on the web page).

Contents

Figures and Tables

Figures

Tables

Summary

The growth of social media as an effective data source for understanding the information environment has made it more important than ever for the U.S. military to develop a robust capacity for social media analytics in support of information operations (IO). Given both the urgency and the challenges in developing such a capacity, and in light of a congressionally mandated assessment, the U.S. Department of Defense (DoD) has a clear need for a research survey of the existing literature on social media analysis technologies, best practices, legal and ethical constraints to social media analysis, and the intersection of IO and social media analytics.

This is a difficult task, however. Existing legal and policy frameworks have not anticipated the rapid pace and global reach of modern communication networks, including social media. There are also technical questions about both the development of a robust social media analysis capacity and the most fruitful applications for these analyses. This report explores these complex issues and offers DoD a set of recommendations for building a social media analysis capability in support of IO that ably and appropriately enhances national security.

How Social Media Analysis Could Support Information Operations

DoD defines *IO* as "the integrated employment, during military operations, of IRCs [information-related capabilities] in concert with other lines of operation to influence, disrupt, corrupt, or usurp the decision making of adversaries and potential adversaries while protecting our own" (Joint Publication [JP] 3-13, 2014). IO can be a component of any type of military operation, and IO planning involves coordinating IRCs—for example, intelligence collection and analysis, military information support operations (MISO), public affairs, or civil-military operations—with other capabilities that generate effects in and through the information environment.

Social media analysis has significant potential to support these operations by providing a window into the perspectives, thoughts, and communications of a wide range of relevant audiences. These platforms can provide important information on a group's or audience's demographics, size, organizational structure, areas of activity, and network reach. Such details can inform efforts to target messages to particular audiences or influence perceptions, decisions, or behavior. In an IO context, for example, social media analysis can identify individuals who are becoming radicalized, measure the prevalence of support for extremist causes among particular demographics, and gauge the depth of this support.

Although social media analysis potentially holds tremendous value for DoD, and social media is undoubtedly an important data source for IO, there are some limitations to leveraging social media platforms and analytic tools. It is important to remember that social media data are not representative of an entire population. Social media's penetration around the world varies, and that is reflected in the available pool of data. Furthermore, the data shared on social media platforms inherently skew toward those who participate. DoD also faces legal restrictions on the collection of data on U.S. persons, so it is essential to implement safeguards to prevent unauthorized access. Finally, there are gray areas in DoD's operational authorities under federal law. Developing a robust social media analysis capacity will first require reexamining IO policies and processes.

To support DoD's assessment of the benefits, trade-offs, and implementation challenges that it will face as it expands its capacity for social media analysis, this report synthesizes research findings from a review of the available literature, supplemented by interviews with subject-matter experts within the DoD IO enterprise and the functional and commercial social media analysis communities. Using this input and applying it to the unique needs and challenges of DoD IO activities, we developed a set of recommendations meant to help DoD navigate this terrain while building a robust, effective social media analytic capability to support operations worldwide.

Recommendations

The following recommendations cover the development of DoD-specific policy and language for social media analysis, doctrinal and institutional issues of implementation, and technology considerations to both usefully analyze social media activity and build up the technological capacity for social media analytics.

Legal Recommendations

A necessary first step in meeting U.S. legal requirements regarding the collection and analysis of social media data—while also effectively meeting national security needs—is to articulate the meaningful difference between military IO under Title 10 of the U.S. Code and foreign intelligence surveillance conducted under Title 50, Executive Order 12333, and the Foreign Intelligence Surveillance Act. Such an articulation should include the following:

- Make clear the relevance of command authority and intent in operations, rather than the methods or source of data, in distinguishing between Title 10 and Title 50 operations.
- Distinguish between "use of force" in conventional operations and the use of nonkinetic IRCs, such as MISO or public affairs.
- Address the complexity of overlapping layers of domestic law and policy that might apply to IO and IRCs, as well as the differences between U.S. and other nations' applicable laws.
- Inform policy and doctrine with clear principles meant to reasonably protect U.S. persons from data collection, and distinguish between operations directed at U.S. persons and operations that may inadvertently collect data on U.S. persons as a by-product of the global reach of modern communication systems and social media.

Develop Title 10–Specific Language for Social Media Analysis

DoD has been using the language and conceptual framework of Title 50 entities while operating under Title 10 authorities. Terms and concepts should be consistent across policies and IO activities:

- In place of the language and (implied) conceptual framework of Title 50 entities, DoD should establish precise, distinct terms of art for social media data acquisition, storage, and analysis, and it should insert that language into doctrine and policy memoranda.

Ethical Recommendations

In addition to ensuring legal compliance in IO, a plausible and sustainable social media analysis capability that meets national security needs must also account for ethical standards in U.S. culture. Our recommendations for ethics considerations include process choices, suggested best practices, and specific recommendations regarding privacy controls:

- Formulate and publish flexible *principles of conduct*, rather than hard-and-fast rules, that accommodate the rapidly evolving nature of social media technologies and trends.
- Whenever possible, make research aims and methods public and explicit while protecting tradecraft and ongoing operations.
- Establish a well-developed and explicit principle of "proportionality" that balances collection intrusiveness against reasonable national security needs.
- Take reasonable safeguards to ensure that methods for storage and distribution of social media data sets—even anonymized ones—protect persons from being identified through cross-referencing or triangulation.
- Develop and publish standards for weighing the risk that collection efforts pose to the free and open use of social media and the Internet against national security benefits.
- Develop and publish a standard on the reasonable expectation of privacy for DoD collection of social media data that balances national security needs and public expectations of transparency.

Recommendations for Implementation and Integration

This report addresses *how* social media analytics could be integrated effectively into DoD IO, as well as *ways* of implementing these approaches. Therefore, we offer the following recommendations concerning DoD's implementation of social media analytics:

- Use the existing IRCs as defined in JP 3-13, *Information Operations* (2014), as a framework for implementing social media analytic approaches.
- Conduct an analysis to determine the potential benefits of a DoD enterprise-level effort to develop social media analytics capacity and capabilities. Such an effort may lead to important cost savings in terms of data collection and analysis, technology acquisition, and training.

Technical Recommendations

Our review of analytic approaches favors existing, open-source technologies and methods. To move forward, DoD must weigh the costs and benefits of using open-source versus commercial solutions. Not all technologies or solutions translate to DoD operational contexts and realities. In particular, DoD should consider the following:

- Carefully weigh the benefits and costs of various tools and workflows. Commercial entities' monetization strategies may work against the government's interest.
- Require access to the underlying processes for collecting and analyzing data. Commercial vendors tend to withhold process information that is critical to ensuring the validity of data analyses in support of IO.

Training and Skill Acquisition

Current training in cyber specialties within DoD is insufficient to support a robust social media analysis capability. To address this shortfall, we offer the following recommendations:

- Given congressional calls for specific policy on the use of social media and other publicly available information, there will be a need for formal training within DoD on oversight and compliance.
- To the degree that DoD chooses to build its social media analysis capacity using military personnel, training should go beyond "buttonology" to teach analysts how to make meaning of social media data.

Table S.1 provides a roadmap for DoD as it continues to explore the factors involved in developing and implementing a social media analysis capability and as it addresses the legal and policy challenges to doing so.

Table S.1
Roadmap for Leveraging Social Media Analysis for DoD IO Campaigns

Action	Outcome
Conduct DoD-level legal review of support for IO by Title 10 organizations.	Update to JP 3-13, Information Operations, that presents clear legal guidance and limitations for commanders and IO planners, including Title 10–specific language for IO-centric data use
Formulate clear guidelines for IO-centric data acquisition, storage, and use within DoD. These guidelines should be informed by similar efforts from academic and industry leaders.	DoD policy memorandum that makes policy guidelines explicit and sets standards for weighing the risks and benefits to national security
Analyze the strengths and weaknesses of DoD's enterprise-level social media analysis capacity, opportunities and costs of its development (including training), and the characteristics of the threats it faces.	Explicit policy decision between either current ad hoc service/combatant command social media analytic efforts or an enterprise-level effort across DoD
Commission an independent review to advise the U.S. government on technology acquisition, focusing on the benefits and trade-offs of open-source versus commercial acquisition strategies.	DoD policy memorandum that outlines criteria for commercial technology acquisition in support of social media analysis

Abbreviations

API	application programming interface
AQAP	al Qaeda in the Arabian Peninsula
DNN	deep neural networks
DoD	U.S. Department of Defense
IDF	Israel Defense Forces
ISIL	Islamic State of Iraq and the Levant
IO	information operations
IRC	information-related capability
JP	joint publication
MILDEC	military deception
MISO	military information support operations
NSA	National Security Agency
OPSEC	operations security
SNA	social network analysis

The Need for Social Media Monitoring to Support U.S. Department of Defense Information Operations

The U.S. Department of Defense (DoD) and the U.S. military services, components, and commands face a difficult challenge in building and operationalizing a social media analysis capability that can support information operations (IO) and other efforts to inform, influence, or persuade.

DoD defines *IO* as "the integrated employment, during military operations, of IRCs [information-related capabilities] in concert with other lines of operation to influence, disrupt, corrupt, or usurp the decision making of adversaries and potential adversaries while protecting our own" (Joint Publication [JP] 3-13, 2014). IO can be a component of any type of military operation and can include efforts to exploit information as a commodity, in addition to technologically driven activities in such areas as cybersecurity, electronic warfare, and operations security (OPSEC). IO planning involves coordinating IRCs—for example, intelligence collection and analysis, military information support operations (MISO), public affairs, or civil-military operations—with other capabilities that generate effects in and through the information environment. This report specifically examines how social media analysis can be applied in ways that support DoD efforts to influence the information environment.

Social media is playing an important and increasing role in IO, because people around world, including civilian populations, U.S. allies, and U.S. adversaries, use social media platforms to share information and persuade others. The rapid growth of the communication technologies that underpin social media platforms has given nonstate adversaries an asymmetric advantage:

> Rapid communications evolutions tend to favor small, agile, less bureaucratic organizations that can more quickly leverage technological advancements without having to negotiate lengthy oversight and authorities processes. The U.S. Department of Defense's advantage in material, financial, and technological resources will be effectively negated if it fails to secure a foothold in these emerging communications spaces. Identification of the most promising techniques and technologies is the crucial first step in positioning to establish relevance in a rapidly changing environment. (Boehnert, 2015, p. 13)

While U.S. adversaries have been quick to exploit this space, DoD lacks the "ability to effectively monitor and utilize social media analytic tools to support awareness of the operating environment for force protection, operational security, and other missions," according to a report by the U.S. House of Representatives Committee on Armed Services on the National Defense Authorization Act for Fiscal Year 2017 (2016, p. 246).

And so, while there are compelling national security reasons to field a social media analysis capability, DoD must do so both while navigating U.S. law and cultural norms and under conditions of great uncertainty. Amid quickly evolving technologies and communication trends, there is a risk that DoD could invest in soon-to-be obsolete capabilities or encounter other challenges in building its analytic capacity and applying it in an effective and practical manner. In addition, as we detail in the next chapter, U.S. law and DoD policy consistently lag behind the technical reality of the rapidly expanding and shifting communication technologies and patterns that have been adopted in such a swift and agile manner by adversaries. This challenge extends beyond U.S. military operations; U.S. academic and research communities grapple with similar uncertainty. However, for DoD, the result is that intelligence units often act without complete clarity about how to legally, ethically, and effectively collect and analyze social media data.

The need for social media analysis tools is so urgent that Congress directed the Secretary of Defense to assess DoD policy on the subject and identify the following:

- demand among U.S. combatant commands for such capabilities, along with a report of current gaps or points where clarification is needed in terms of policy, doctrine, training, and technological capabilities
- operational missions in which social media analysis is needed, with examples including battlespace awareness, OPSEC, counter-messaging, and the operational use of publicly available information[1]
- the legal and policy issues associated with the use of publicly available information
- resource limitations, approval processes, and training requirements affecting DoD's use of publicly available information, as well as steps the department is taking to improve coordination and leverage best practices and capabilities
- DoD plans to ensure that operations do not violate the privacy of U.S. persons and that safeguards are in place to prevent unauthorized access to information (U.S. House of Representatives, Committee on Armed Services, 2016, p. 241).

---

[1] The recently published DoD Manual 5240.01, *Procedures Governing the Conduct of DoD Intelligence Activities*, defines *publicly available information* as follows:

> Information that has been published or broadcast for public consumption, is available on request to the public, is accessible on-line or otherwise to the public, is available to the public by subscription or purchase, could be seen or heard by any casual observer, is made available at a meeting open to the public, or is obtained by visiting any place or attending any event that is open to the public. Publicly available information includes information generally available to persons in a military community even though the military community is not open to the civilian general public. (DoD Manual 5240.01, 2016, p. 53)

Purpose and Scope of This Report

Given both the urgency and the challenges in developing a social media analysis capability, and in light of a congressionally mandated assessment, DoD's counterterrorism technical support office requested a research survey of the existing literature on social media analysis technologies, best practices, legal and ethical constraints to social media analysis, and the intersection of IO and social media analysis. This report synthesizes research findings with the aims of mapping the "terrain" of issues DoD will face in the near future as it develops plans to operationalize new social media analysis technologies and techniques and offering context for informed discussion of these plans and their outcomes. Based on a review of the available literature as well as interviews with subject-matter experts, we offer a set of recommendations meant to help DoD navigate this terrain while building a robust, effective social media analytic capability to support operations worldwide.

To enhance both the utility and longevity of the findings of this study, the substantive chapters of this report address social media analysis in a general and approach-based manner. Even as social media technologies and platforms change, the concepts and practices should remain relevant to DoD's mission.

This report specifically addresses the U.S. military's use of social media analysis in support of IO, such as the use of social media data to better understand local attitudes and concerns in a given area. It does not cover the use of social media as a broadcast platform from which to conduct IO—for example, using microblogs to attempt to persuade local populations to support U.S. military operations.

Of course, social media is just a subset of a much larger universe of publicly available information (see DoD Manual 5240.01, 2016). DoD policy and the department's social media analysis capacity are bound within the larger issue of how to handle publicly available information, and we acknowledge the value of this information. For example, self-reported mobile device usage patterns or users' preference for a certain type of device might help analysts better understand the information environment in a given area. How to best use publicly available information is a subject worthy of further study. However, this report specifically examines social media analysis, not publicly available information and its use writ large.

Study Approach and Methods

This report synthesizes findings from relevant research on social media analytic concepts, applications, and challenges, as well as the literature on IO writ large. Literature sources were primarily academic and DoD-sponsored research, but they also included legal journals, industry reports, and some journalistic sources. We also drew on literature from academic research communities that are, themselves, wrestling with practices and rules that do not account for social media as a novel location for research. Subsequent chapters feature examples from these studies that are relevant to IO.

We supplemented our research by conducting five interviews with subject-matter experts within the DoD IO enterprise and the functional and commercial social media analysis communities. Our goal was to identify analytic practices, means, and concerns that are currently or potentially relevant to DoD's IO mission. Our interviews do not represent a generalizable sample of expert perspectives, but they do offer an operationally grounded perspective from uniformed and civilian IO personnel from across DoD with significant experience in the approaches and challenges addressed in this report. The interviews were confidential to encourage these experts to speak freely and draw on their personal perspectives and experience. Because these interviews were meant to elicit specific technical information, not generalizable knowledge, RAND's Institutional Review Board found that our project did not constitute human subjects research.

Structure of This Report

The remainder of this report explores how DoD can begin thinking about implementing social media analysis in support of IO. The discussion is supplemented by many examples of how these approaches could be used in particular IO contexts, the limitations on the use of these data, and the legal and policy frameworks under which DoD must operate.

Chapter Two argues that social media analysis is essential to conducting IO effectively now and into the future. Because social media analysis is a relatively new concept, we frame the discussion in terms of IRCs, with which the IO community is already familiar. The chapter then presents a framework for thinking about and applying social media analytic approaches, along with example applications for various IRCs.

Chapter Three provides an overview of current best practices and analytic approaches, but the discussion is not limited to current technology. Drawing on RAND's expertise and leadership in social media analysis and analytics, the chapter focuses on the utility of text and image data for IO and methods that can maximize this utility. We also present a conceptual model for thinking about levels of analysis of social media data and how each level of analysis can inform IO.

Chapter Four examines U.S. legal and ethical frameworks for social media analysis and challenges for IO, in particular, providing context for nontechnical questions of social media use as part of IO.

Chapter Five concludes this report with a series of recommendations for implementing social media analysis in a way that supports DoD's mission and meets oversight requirements. The recommendations are provider-agnostic in terms of support and acquisition to ensure that they are applicable to a range of activities and initiatives. The chapter also includes recommendations related to U.S. legal and ethical requirements, building social media analysis capacity to support IO, and the dissemination of social media analytical products.

CHAPTER TWO

How Social Media Analysis Could Support Information Operations

Social media analysis has significant potential to support DoD information operations because it provides a window into the perspectives, thoughts, and communications of a wide range of relevant audiences. Both organizations and individual users contribute to potentially rich social media data sets through their public postings. For example, social media platforms can provide important information on a group or audience's demographics, size, organizational structure, areas of activity, and network reach. Such details can inform efforts to target messages to particular audiences or influence the perceptions, decisions, or behavior of a group. This information is particularly relevant to IO when it pertains to groups that are essential to the outcome of military operations, whether the group is an adversary, a supporting community on either side of a conflict, or necessary to support the desired end state of an information campaign.

For example, text analysis can be used to identify individuals who are becoming radicalized, measure the prevalence of support for extremist causes among particular demographics, and gauge the depth of this support (Correa and Sureka, 2013). Geotagged posts can supplement social media analysis, helping IO practitioners identify the geographic spread of ideas or areas of particularly strong or weak support for a cause, group, or idea. Network analysis provides additional potential benefits in planning efforts to promote or counter the spread of specific ideas or information. Analyzing the data generated by social media posts against metadata and the demographics of users associated with the accounts can help identify influencers in a social network, allowing information campaigns to target the groups or individuals who are most amenable to influence. Image classification algorithms can aggregate and describe the kinds of images shared on social media, which, when analyzed alongside other data with geoinferencing and mapping software, could allow IO practitioners to visualize changes in local populations' preferences and attitudes.

In this chapter, we examine the potential of social media analysis to inform and support IO. We use the IRCs as an existing framework, showing how social media analysis can be used as both a data source and a set of analytic methods across several IRCs. IO and the IRCs are familiar concepts to IO practitioners and are features of DoD doctrine. In this way, we use IRCs as a framework to link new methods and technologies to current DoD practice.

Social media analysis can help DoD IO practitioners better understand adversary intelligence collection efforts, identify networks of interest, and gather intelligence remotely at fairly granular levels. It also has applications in efforts to gauge public opinion, measure and detect adversary influence operations, and influence tradecraft. Both OPSEC and military deception (MILDEC) campaigns can be revised if social media analysis detects OPSEC violations or indicators that deception has failed and thus protect sensitive information from potential adversaries. Finally, we examine how social media analysis can support public affairs efforts, help leverage civil-military operations, and facilitate key leader engagement.

The Information Environment and Information-Related Capabilities

The increased use of electronic communication and information sharing has both enhanced the ability to communicate and quickly share large amounts of data and introduced new vulnerabilities. These vulnerabilities affect each of the physical, informational, and cognitive dimensions of the information environment outlined in JP 3-13. Figure 2.1 visualizes these dimensions as distinct but interrelated. For example, a loss of informational capability could have significant

Figure 2.1
Components of the Information Environment

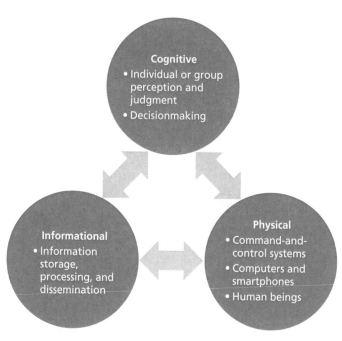

SOURCE: Derived from JP 3-13, 2014.
RAND RR1742-2.1

effects on decisionmaking in the cognitive sphere and the functioning of network architectures in the physical sphere.

IRCs are the tools and activities that a commander uses to reduce vulnerabilities and to exploit and affect adversaries in the information environment. In this report, we focus on the IRCs to which social media data are most applicable, particularly intelligence, influence (MISO), OPSEC, MILDEC, public affairs, civil-military operations, and key leader engagement. Table 2.1 summarizes how these IRCs are defined in DoD doctrine.

The remainder of this chapter reviews each IRC and provides examples of how social media analysis could inform and enhance these capabilities.

Table 2.1
IRC Types and Definitions

IRC	Definition
Intelligence	Provides "population-centric sociocultural intelligence and physical network lay downs, including the information transmitted via those networks"
MISO	"planned operations to convey selected information and indicators to foreign audiences to influence their emotions, motives, objective reasoning, and ultimately the behavior of foreign governments"
OPSEC	"standardized process designed to meet operational needs by mitigating risks associated with specific vulnerabilities in order to deny adversaries critical information and observable indicators"
MILDEC	"actions executed to deliberately mislead adversary decision makers"
Public affairs	"public information, command information, and public engagement activities directed toward both the internal and external publics with interest in DoD"
Civil-military operations	operations to "establish, maintain, influence, or exploit relations between military forces, governmental and nongovernmental civilian organizations and authorities, and the civilian populace in a friendly, neutral, or hostile operational area in order to achieve US objectives"
Key leader engagement	"engagements that can be used to shape and influence foreign leaders at the strategic, operational, and tactical levels"

SOURCE: JP 3-13, 2014.

Intelligence

The volume and range of information posted to social media make these platforms both a challenging and ideal place for intelligence collection. For example, Twitter users alone post 500 million tweets every day (Oreskovic, 2015). Users post photos, videos, and status updates to social media, and their profiles often include such personal details as their age, gender, family members, and place of employment. These posts offer insight into the daily lives of individuals, as well as the attitudes and behaviors of social networks. It is now common practice for major companies to use social media analytics to better understand their customer base, guiding marketing decisions and product development (interview with subject-matter expert, September 1, 2016). Companies use services like Topsy (acquired by Apple in 2013) and Sprinklr to analyze social media data and inform strategies to engage customers and better target their marketing efforts. These services provide in-depth analyses of the audiences that view the companies' posts and how those audiences engage with both the company and others online. The ability to compile data from across sources can produce extremely valuable analysis, and this was a recurring theme in our expert interviews.

The past several years have provided multiple examples of social media data as a source for valuable intelligence for both government and commercial entities. A geotagged post on a fighter's social media account drew the attention of a U.S. Air Force unit, which used the information to launch a bombing campaign on a headquarters building belonging to the Islamic State in Iraq and the Levant (ISIL) in 2015 (see Everstine, 2015). Shipping companies have used Twitter and Facebook posts by Somali pirates to better understand how criminal organizations target ships and plan their attacks (Lahe, 2012). Machine learning and other methods used to process the large amounts of information posted on social media can enhance the security community's real-time collection of data on security threats and events, improving forecasting of future areas of instability. These data can also provide insights into criminal or terrorist group activities and help identify members and where they gather.

Understanding Networks by Analyzing Social Media Data

In their most basic form, maps of individual user relationships and interactions on social media platforms can identify members of a particular group. Researchers have been able to detect nuances in the dynamics of interpersonal networks by analyzing the information posted by users on these platforms. Examining follower relationships on Twitter, researchers were able to map opinion networks based on foreign policy discussions of the Iran-Israel confrontation over Iran's nuclear program (Zeitzoff, Kelly, and Lotan, 2015). These online opinion networks reflected offline policy differences, providing a valuable method for identifying members of different opinion groups. This research has implications beyond simple opinion networks; it can also be used to identify individuals who are radicalizing or likely to commit a crime.

There is particular value in the ability of social media data to reveal regional trends. Researchers found that when there were large increases in Iranians' discussion about an event or issue on social media but no corresponding increase in posts in other countries, the issue was not picked up by major news outlets (Zeitzoff, Kelly, and Lotan, 2015). Country- or region-specific changes in public opinion or deviations in the language and tone used to discuss an issue could be valuable information in a conflict environment.

A recent Brookings Institution report shows how social media and network analysis might be used to gather information on a targeted organization. The authors analyzed a sample of 20,000 user accounts on Twitter expressing support for ISIL, extracting information on the location and activity level of the supporters, the languages most often used in their tweets, and the number of Twitter users following these accounts. They found that much of the group's success could be attributed to a relatively small number of very active users in Syria, Iraq, and other areas contested by ISIL (Berger and Morgan, 2015).

A RAND report provides an even more detailed analysis of ISIL's Twitter network. *Daesh* is an Arabic term generally used in the Middle East by those who oppose the group, while supporters use variations of *Islamic State*. Using these terms to distinguish the accounts of users who supported ISIL from those who opposed the group, the authors were able to conduct a network analysis of each opposing camp and evaluate how these groups interacted with each other (Bodine-Baron, Marcellino, et al., 2015). Evaluating who interacts with ISIL supporters and how often could be valuable in increasing understanding of the group and identifying key influencers, or those most capable of swaying supporters away from ISIL. As in the Brookings study, RAND's analysis of geotagged tweets yielded insights into the geographic spread of ISIL supporters. In these ways, the information that social media provides can supplement and inform intelligence collection and analysis.

Verifying the Credibility and Accuracy of Social Media Data

Social media has been used to immediately crowdsource verification of developments and events, improving situational awareness for security forces. When major events occur, users are likely to post about them on social media, turning even passive bystanders into "citizen journalists, providing and relaying information from the ground," often in real time (Omand, Bartlett, and Miller, 2012). During the riots in London and other English cities in the aftermath of a 2011 police shooting and alleged cover-up, for example, the police created an online platform that allowed citizens to post updates on the situation in their communities and identify those who engaged in looting and violence from a collection of photos of suspects posted by law enforcement. Analysis of Twitter traffic during this time found that bursts of tweets often preempted traditional news reports about a major event (Omand, Bartlett, and Miller, 2012). Law enforcement agencies were able to use this information to improve their situational awareness and respond to events more quickly. While this form of engagement goes beyond simple monitoring, one could imagine a similar effort in which IO practitioners analyze social media data on a riot unfolding in a country in which U.S. forces are operating, using these data to plan interventions to diminish the spread of disorder, identify agitators, and perhaps expose, shame, influence, or arrest specific individuals.

While social media data have a clear sampling bias—analysts can assess only the information that users choose to make public, and social media users tend to be young, urban, and well educated—these data do have the potential to provide valuable insights into events as they happen. The demanding process of extracting relevant, useful data from the enormous amount of information posted to social media platforms can be mitigated by employing software specifically designed to filter posts for human analysts or machine learning systems that can directly perform these types of analyses. Software that can conduct credibility analysis of social media posts already exists, and it has helped reduce the amount of irrelevant information that human end users must parse. Such software also uses sentiment analysis to identify pro- or anti-government accounts and can map social networks for both sides using this information (Kase et al., 2014). Such software is not yet able to analyze tweets themselves, and problems arise when computer programs encounter nuances in language and culture. However, it does reduce the amount of information that an IO practitioner is required to review, and it provides richer context for analysis. Researchers anticipate that machine learning could be used to conduct sentiment analysis of protest crowds in the future, gauging the mood and propensity for violence at any given time (Omand, Bartlett, and Miller, 2012).

Social media has been used successfully by governments and their adversaries to monitor and collect intelligence on both individual citizens and networked groups. While the extent of U.S. involvement in these activities has been limited, the information gleaned from social media could be extremely valuable in intelligence preparation of the battlefield. In urban centers, in particular, social media is an ideal source of information on an area of operations. Social media network and text analysis can provide insight into the social and cultural aspects of the information environment and identify changes. As sentiment and credibility analysis improves, the speed and reliability of applications and the information they collect will increase.

Military Information Support Operations

Social media has been used extensively by both governments and nonstate actors to influence public opinion in areas of conflict. In operational environments, DoD has a need and responsibility to detect and counter the propaganda efforts of adversaries and potential adversaries. The United States has launched many such campaigns in the past, but the fast-moving nature of social media requires different techniques to quickly identify, monitor, and counter adversaries' influence operations. Studies have found that public opinion on Twitter develops and then stabilizes into a dominant opinion very quickly, giving the greatest advantage to large groups that are able to shape opinion early on (Xiong and Liu, 2014). Research using computer simulations of interpersonal influence processes has found that the formation of public opinion is driven by a "critical mass of easily influenced individuals"

(Watts and Dodds, 2007), making social media and the ease with which it allows information to be shared an ideal resource for propagating ideas. It is critical for DoD to understand the extent to which both governments and nonstate actors use social media to influence public opinion, as well as their success in doing so.

Social Media and Influence Operations

Monitoring social media networks and the progress of changing sentiments gives military planners an opportunity to better understand how and where these actors are working to influence public opinion. These data can then inform efforts to counter their campaigns, but they also reveal the issues that adversaries find most important. Social media is unique in its ability to rapidly spread images, though these images are often misleading or posted without context. A single photo or short video can act as a powerful device to alter how the public conceptualizes an issue. Groups like ISIL have been relatively successful in taking advantage of social media at the ground level in Syria, shaping the narrative of the conflict and public opinion by disseminating biased and curated imagery that appears to be raw material posted by individual users (Zeitzoff, Kelly, and Lotan, 2015). Both China and Russia have actively used social media in this way in large-scale, coordinated campaigns. China employs thousands of people to post pro-government propaganda and promote the agenda of the party on message boards and blogs (Drapeau and Wells, 2009). Russia similarly pays people to post pro-government content and criticize opponents in chat rooms and the comments sections of news articles (Khazan, 2013).

The use of social media by Hezbollah and Hamas has been written about extensively, as both of the groups are particularly skilled at using social media to craft narratives in conflict areas. When Israel launched an airstrike against Hezbollah during the 2006 Lebanon War, the group edited photos of victims and recovery workers to make the attack appear genocidal rather than military in nature (Keller, 2010). The use of social media to influence public opinion was also part of a larger strategy to force the hand of the Israel Defense Forces (IDF). Hezbollah's social media campaign was described as "a stage-managed Hizballah production, designed precisely to enflame [sic] international sentiment against Israel and compel the Israelis to accept a ceasefire that would enable the jihad terrorist group to gain some time to recover from the Israeli attacks" (Spencer, 2006). As both sides launched social media propaganda campaigns, individuals and nongovernmental organizations, including Human Rights Watch and Amnesty International, alleged human rights violations by the IDF, calling for action from the international community.

The exclusion of foreign reporters from war zones only adds to the impact of social media campaigns. During the Gaza conflict in 2006, Israel attempted to keep media out of the area of operations. International media outlets whose reporters were barred from entering the area found a blog belonging to a Gazan recent college graduate, and it soon became their primary source of information on the developing situation on the ground. Sameh Habeeb updated his blog daily and provided news outlets with reports on casualties, attacks, and the general situation in Gaza. Major media outlets, including CNN, BBC, and Le Monde, came to rely on Habeeb's reports and featured them in their broadcasts (Gilinsky, 2009).

Other Gazans similarly acted as citizen journalists, using You-Tube, Twitter, and blogs to share video and photos from the conflict zone. With international journalists prevented from reporting directly on the situation in Gaza, media outlets were left to settle for images that lacked context or were accompanied by unverifiable claims. Many of these posts served to reinforce Palestinian reports of atrocities committed by the IDF.

To help counter the influence of these activities, Israel organized its own teams of citizen-reporters, and the IDF disseminated footage of its aerial bombings on its YouTub channel, emphasizing that it was at war with Hamas, not Gaza's civilian population. Hamas also launched an information campaign, with statistics contradicting those released by the IDF and other information intended to sway international opinion (Gilinsky, 2009). In such a complex information environment, social media analysis could help governments anticipate when and how influence operations will be used, allowing IO practitioners to prevent the dissemination of false information and facilitate faster responses when such information is released.

In areas of interest to the United States, it is not only adversaries that engage in influence operations; nonstate groups trying to counter extremism and violence use social media as well. For example, in 2008, a group of students in Colombia created the Facebook group "One Million Voices Against the FARC (Revolutionary Armed Forces of Colombia)," posting documents and videos of hostages held in harsh conditions. The story was picked up by international media outlets, leading 6 million people around the world to march against the FARC and successfully pressure the group to release more hostages (Gendron, Blas-Irizarry, and Boggs, 2009).

As news outlets compete to broadcast events before their competitors, they draw on social media campaigns and bring international attention to these causes. In this way, one individual's images have the potential to influence public opinion on an issue worldwide. There is a clear need for analytic tools to monitor influence operations and the effects of social media on a large scale. Such analyses would serve as a powerful mechanism for verifying user reports and informing appropriate responses.

The Critical Importance of Influence Operations

We cannot stress enough how critical influence operations are to mission success. Everything that DoD does—or fails to do—operationally has an effect on the information environment. And because U.S. military action across a continuum of operations is likely to be actively contested by those opposed to U.S. interests, military commanders and planners must account for social media's impact on audiences. The examples presented in this chapter underscore the importance of U.S. monitoring and analysis of influence operations through social media, but the important conclusion is that, very often, popular support is a key factor in mission success. By using social media *analysis* to better understand how states and nonstate actors are using social media to influence public opinion, commanders can better anticipate and encourage civil support on the battlefield, as well as identify possible constraints on the use of force.

Monitoring social media activity could prevent these incidents or allow faster response times by law enforcement.

Deducing Sensitive Details from Publicly Available Information

Social media analysis has the potential to identify OPSEC risks resulting from the exposure of personally identifiable information. Until 2011, the last four digits of a service member's social security number could be found on public websites (Phillips and Pickett, 2011). While seemingly innocuous, the public disclosure of small amounts of sensitive information can be sufficient to construct a larger profile of a target, allowing a malicious actor to link these details to individuals and exploit this knowledge to compromise the identity and security of DoD employees and service members. Inputting a few key pieces of information on one individual into a search engine can provide access to home addresses, phone numbers, and information on family members. Further details available on social media pages can provide answers to "secret questions" to access account pages and other critical information. Simply searching the membership of Facebook groups associated with military units can help adversaries identify service members associated with the units and their personal networks. As facial recognition software becomes more advanced, it could be used to associate official military photographs with the personal photos and social media pages of service members.

Revealing Sensitive Information in Social Media Posts

Service members and their families are frequently asked not to post sensitive information, such as deployment dates and locations, on social media, but it is currently impossible for DoD to monitor such a large number of social media accounts. However, using an automated or human-in-the-loop approach to monitoring these accounts for sensitive information would be highly valuable from an OPSEC perspective. The demands of monitoring the social media accounts of an aircraft carrier crew of 5,000 are multiplied when friends and family members are entrusted with information on the movements of their loved ones. As service members post photos and updates and family members share information, there is an increased risk that privacy controls will fail or a user will share sensitive information with a malicious actor.

There have been several instances of social media postings compromising OPSEC. In 2010, IDF was forced to postpone an operation after a soldier posted the location and time of a planned raid on his personal Facebook page (Katz, 2010). In 2009, Representative Peter Hoekstra, a member of the House Intelligence Committee, tweeted his location and activities every few hours while on sensitive travel to Iraq, endangering both himself and his travel companions (Levin, 2015).

Geotagging has emerged as a particularly dangerous threat to OPSEC, as many users are not aware that geotags are automatically embedded in photos taken with mobile devices. Returning to a previously mentioned example, Air Force General Herbert "Hawk" Carlisle recently demonstrated the enormous utility of geotagged social media posts when his unit pinpointed the location of an ISIL headquarters building based on a geotagged post by an ISIL militant. The unit destroyed the structure with three joint direct attack munitions a mere 22 hours later (Everstine, 2015). Conversely, geotagged photos or posts on social media can pose a risk to U.S. forces by exposing unit locations and patterns of movement both in a conflict zone and at home.

Awareness of the availability of publicly available information and methods to prevent its spread is important to protecting service members and OPSEC. Training for service members that draws on findings from social media analysis can improve OPSEC practices and enforce service members' understanding of the ease with which personal information can be deduced from postings. On an organizational level, this type of analysis can better inform DoD's own prevention efforts.

Public Affairs

DoD has struggled to balance IO demands and public affairs needs, going so far as to shut down its Office of Strategic Influence after a *New York Times* article accused it of "propagandizing the American public" (Opperman, 2012). As evidenced by previous examples in this chapter, however, adversaries' ability to quickly spread information and propaganda has only continued to increase.

Although DoD has worked to implement its social media strategies in support of public affairs campaigns, U.S. adversaries' continued use of social media necessitates that it expand these strategies to enable it to track and collect information on adversary activities. The competing information campaigns of the IDF, Hamas, and Hezbollah have demonstrated the confusion that can occur when military conflicts are accompanied by a battle for information dominance on social media platforms. Similarly, the spread of false reports of violence against Muslims near Assam, India, reveals the ease with which a small number of individuals can influence perceptions and foster this type of confusion. The public affairs efforts of terrorist groups are most often categorized as "propaganda," but these groups commit considerable time and resources to disseminating information, messages, and multimedia. In some cases, traditional media networks, lacking their own firsthand reporting, have used videos produced by terrorist groups in their broadcasts, often without disclaimers to identify the source (Dauber, 2009).

A more agile and proactive DoD public affairs strategy can mitigate some of the influence of these adversary campaigns. From a DoD-centric perspective, public affairs organizations are well positioned to inform social media analysis efforts aimed at OPSEC or force protection. Monitoring the use of enemy propaganda through social media analysis to isolate how, when, and where it is being deployed can help target public affairs efforts in more timely and effective ways. It can also reveal where traditional media outlets lack coverage, reducing the reliance on unreliable or biased observers for reports from conflict areas. Given that DoD public affairs organizations are active in digital spaces, for example running readiness groups on social media, and should be integrated into information operations writ large, public affairs officers' access to analytic tools and methods could powerfully leverage their efforts.

Civil-Military Operations

There has been little research on the use of social media in supporting civil-military operations, but there is great potential for social media analysis to inform and leverage these efforts. Humanitarian aid organizations have embraced social media as a tool to improve their operations. Many of their methods could be transferred to a conflict environment. OpenStreetMaps, an open-source collective dedicated to developing a detailed map of the world, recruited volunteers to create and share layouts of Haiti's previously unmapped neighborhoods for use by aid workers (Nelson, 2011). Facebook and other social media platforms have been used to create "crisis maps," alerting aid workers to areas in need of assistance (Goolsby, 2013). The use of social media to report injuries and characterize the situation on the ground provided aid organizations with the information needed for a timely response in the wake of the 2011 earthquake and tsunami in Japan (Abbasi et al., 2011). TweetTracker, a tool that uses a Twitter-streaming application programming interface (API) to retrieve, store, and analyze tweets, provides valuable analysis for humanitarian assistance/disaster relief operations (Kumar et al., 2011). Its features include interactive visualizations of geolocated tweets on topics of interest, along with data summaries, translation options, and trend tracking and comparisons.

The information-sharing and crowdsourcing dimensions of social media could help commanders target specific communities or areas for civil-military liaison efforts during counterinsurgency operations. Social media monitoring could also supplement face-to-face liaison activities as these operations progress. Using crisis maps, public sentiment analysis, and other types of social media data collection and analysis, commanders and staff planners could measure the effectiveness and impact of specific information campaigns or civil-military operations more broadly.

Key Leader Engagement

DoD has struggled to develop a policy that encourages the use of social media while maintaining OPSEC. This lack of guidance has made commanders reluctant to use social media, thereby allowing social media–savvy terrorist groups to spread their ideas and narratives, often without significant counterinformation campaigns by the United States. Timothy Cunningham, a deputy program manager at the Director of National Intelligence Open Source Center, described the problem as rooted in DoD's reliance on old media and its one-way flow of information rather than taking advantage of the interactive nature of new media (Schoen, 2011).

Just as there is in MISO, we think there is tremendous potential for social media analytic approaches to inform key leader engagement. In Chapter Three, we outline some approaches that could provide commanders with an efficient means to gain insight into public sentiment and the concerns of local populations, as well as detect and unpack the argument strategies circulated by and among key influencers. This sort of bottom-up, data-driven analysis could help commanders avoid "mirroring" errors in communication and develop engagement strategies that will resonate with key leaders.[1]

An IRC-Based Framework for Building Social Media Analytic Capacity

This chapter began with a discussion of highly generalizable concepts, proposing an IRC-based framework for integrating social media analytics and IO. Subsequent discussion provided an orientation to some operational applications for analytic tools, accompanied by examples and brief overviews of potential benefits and risks. Chapter Three explores the utility of social media analysis with greater specificity, presenting an illustrative set of methodological approaches to solving particular IO problems with social media data.

---

[1]   *Mirroring* refers to projecting values, goals, and norms on a target audience.

Table 2.2 provides an overview of the methodological approaches that apply to each IRC, including social network analysis (SNA), publics analysis, lexical analysis, stance analysis, geolocation and geoinferencing, and deep neural networks (DNN). Chapter Three discusses these approaches and how they can be applied in greater detail. Many of the approaches are even more valuable when used in combination with others. As mentioned earlier, a social media post showing a hangar bay full of aircraft has the potential to seriously harm OPSEC. Using DNN to automatically identify the types of aircraft in the images and geolocation to determine where the photograph was taken could help commanders identify sensitive information and prevent its accidental spread. As the use of social media evolves, various approaches will become more or less valuable to particular IRCs.

Table 2.2
IRCs and Methodological Approaches

IRC	Applicable Methodological Approaches
Intelligence	SNA, lexical analysis, stance analysis, geolocation, DNN
MISO	Publics analysis, lexical analysis, stance analysis, geolocation
OPSEC and MILDEC	Geolocation, DNN
Public affairs	Publics analysis, lexical analysis, stance analysis
Civil-military operations	Publics analysis, lexical analysis, stance analysis, geolocation
Key leader engagement	Publics analysis, lexical analysis, stance analysis

CHAPTER THREE

Social Media Analytical Methods for Supporting Information Operations

In the previous chapter, we presented an IRC-based framework for thinking about the potential benefits of applying social media analysis to IO. In this chapter, we move to a more specific set of illustrations: methodological approaches to measuring popular reception of an extremist group's propaganda, identifying cultural or regional concerns in support of messaging strategies, and solving other IO problems. This chapter does not focus on specific technologies or algorithms; such discussions of *means* can rapidly become outdated. Rather, we explore some promising *ways* to address common IO challenges within a familiar framework. For example, popular community-detection algorithms, such as Clauset-Newman Moore, may be supplanted by superior options, but the need to distinguish and analyze communities within a social network is enduring.

Social Media's Limitations as Data Source

The concepts and approaches surveyed in this chapter potentially hold tremendous value for DoD, and social media is undoubtedly an important data source for IO. However, there are some limitations to leveraging social media platforms and analytic tools:

- Social media penetration is variable around the world, and this is reflected in the amount of data available for analysis (and their applicability) in a given area of operation.

- Social media data are not representative. Participants are self-selected, and, thus, the data they share inherently skew toward the populations that participate.

So, for example, analysis of automated image classification data derived from photos shared on social media reveals what a subset of a population thinks is worth sharing,

Key Concepts and Methods in Social Media Analysis

The example analyses that follow are not exhaustive, but they have been chosen to show the range of possible approaches and to illustrate the value of combined approaches that use multiple analytic methods. And while the majority of approaches use textual analysis (reflecting the abundance of text-based data in social media), we have also included examples involving network, geospatial, and imagery analysis.

Key methodological concepts in this chapter include the following:

- *Social network analysis.* SNA, which involves identifying and visualizing social structures, draws on work in the fields of psychology, anthropology, and graph theory in mathematics (Scott, 2012). It includes algorithms for the automated detection of communities in large social media data sets.
- *Publics.* Publics are a unit of analysis in public persuasion: abstractions of people with an advocacy stake using shared language to address a common problem. The National Rifle Association is a real-world example of an organization involved in advocacy, but the public that uses similar language and shares a goal of legitimizing private ownership of weapons is a much larger abstraction. The opposing public that seeks to limit the ownership of weapons is also larger than any formal lobbying group. This type of analysis focuses on the set of people who care about an issue and use a shared discourse to affect debate.

- *Lexical analysis.* Text analysis approaches were developed in corpus linguistics studies.[1] Lexical analysis uses statistical tests to count word frequencies, word distance, and other characteristics to detect structure and patterns in text data. It is used most frequently to empirically determine what a text collection is about, through conspicuously over- and underpresent words, and word connections.
- *Stance analysis.* A more sophisticated and granular kind of sentiment analysis, stance analysis examines frequencies of *categories* of words and phrases (e.g., anger, sadness, future, past, certainty, uncertainty). It is useful for answering sociocultural questions about attitudes, affect, and values.
- *Geolocation and geoinferencing.* These are two geo-specific methods for determining the geographic origin of a social media message. Geolocation uses GPS stamping and is highly accurate; however, users often turn this feature off. Geoinferencing can capture a larger data sample by using metadata to make inferences about the geographic location of posters, and some methods have high levels of accuracy.
- *Deep neural networks.* DNNs allow machines to learn categorization tasks by reducing complex abstractions to simple layers. For example, whereas a human might look at a picture and holistically recognize a tank, a DNN image classifier might be programmed to differentiate metal texture, tread shapes, a main gun shape, a low reflective value, and other factors to categorize a "tank" with a reasonable level of accuracy. Instead of a human analyst spending a year searching through hundreds of thousands of images, a well-trained DNN model with sufficient computing power might require only days to categorize that same set of images.

---

[1] Corpus linguistics is a subdiscipline of linguistics characterized by the empirical study of very large text data sets (*corpora*). Because corpus linguistics is machine-based, it lacks the precision and context-sensitivity of human analysis, but human analysis cannot match its scalability and reliability.

Approaches to Analyzing Social Media Data

While social media data increasingly include images, sound, and video, textual data still predominate. In the following sections, we review various social media analytic approaches—particularly those using text data—that have real-world applicability in solving IO problems. Table 3.1 summarizes the approaches discussed in this chapter and example applications.

Network Description: Uncovering Extremist Networks in Social Media

While this chapter focuses primarily on analytic methods, we note the value in descriptive work that can provide important insight through inference. This section details a method for characterizing extremist networks—specifically, the network members who are actively engaged in support activities.[2] In this example, the goal was to describe active supporters of ISIL on Twitter, but the approach could be applied

Table 3.1
Selected Approaches to Analyzing Social Media Data in Support of IO Campaigns

Approach	Example Application
Network description	Descriptive analysis of extremist networks using hand-curated seed lists to extrapolate and track support networks
Publics analysis	Lexical and network analysis to detect, characterize, and map networked communities of users who engage with each other through social media
Resonance analysis	Lexical and statistical measures of the spread and uptake of extremist messaging over time and geographically
Stance analysis	Digital analysis of tradecraft in messaging
Automated image analysis	Geospatial detection and mapping of imagery shared over social media using DNN image classification and geolocation/inferencing

---

[2]   Different analytic approaches would be useful in examining general conversation *about* the group on social media.

to other networked groups or social media platforms that make data available for SNA.

In this example approach, existing ISIL supporters were used to identify other supporters. The result was a fairly large data set of between 1 million and 1.35 million active ISIL supporters on Twitter (Berger and Morgan, 2015). Identifying members of the network was a three-step process that combined machine approaches for scalability with human-supervised random sample checks for accuracy.

Using Seed Accounts to Identify Network Members

The first step in the process was developing a hand-curated seed list of known extremist members who were active on Twitter. This is a labor-intensive process even for experts (on the order of months for a two-person team). In their manual search of accounts that indicated active support for an extremist group in users' Twitter activity, researchers identified 424 active ISIL supporters—or level 0 in the network model.

The second step was to use assortative network connections to infer other supporters, starting from the seed list. Unlike other approaches that use content to identify affiliation (see the following section, "Publics Analysis: Mapping the Argument Space on Social Media"), here, the direction of the connection matters. Imagine a group of Twitter users commenting on a popular TV show. Participants in these interactions might include cast members, production crew, studio representatives, journalists, and, of course, fans of the show. If we have identified members of the show's network—stars, the writers, the showrunner, and so on—we can then make likely guesses about the other users who are talking about the show by analyzing the directionality of their connections: The star may have many, many followers (mostly fans) who are not directly related to the show, but the people whom the star *follows* are much more likely to be affiliated with the show.

Thus, in the extremist network example, ignoring those who follow the level 0 seed members and instead identifying those *followed by* level 0 seed members gives a potentially more accurate picture of likely network members (level 1). In this example, after a pass to remove suspected bots and spam, this one-step group in the network numbered approximately 43,000 users. But, of course, not all the people followed by level 0 members are Twitter supporters of ISIL; further culling is required.

Using Cliquishness and In-Network Focus to Improve Network Membership Identification

A third step in identifying network members who actively support ISIL was to sort the remaining 43,000 users in the data set by their overt engagement with ISIL on Twitter, as well as their degree of cliquishness and in-network focus. In network analysis, these concepts are defined as follows:

- *Cliques* are substructures within a network in which every node is connected to every other node. Imagine a large network of supporters for the New England Patriots. Within that network structure, you might find many small cliques—groups in which everyone knows everyone else. They might be a tight group of friends from a neighborhood in Boston, or they also might have never met face to face but know each other through their online interactions. What matters is the degree of cliquishness, which helps indicate membership in the network.
- *In-network focus* refers to the tendency to have more in-network connections than out-of-network connections (interactions with users outside a group). In our football example, even casual fans of the New England Patriots may have a few in-network connections, but if someone's ratio of network connections skews in—if a user is primarily pointed inward at the network—that indicates strength of membership.

Sorting the 43,000 level 1 accounts using these combined metrics proved to be much more accurate than using a single metric to identify supporters. When spot-checked by a human analyst, this approach showed very high accuracy (93 percent) for the top 20,000 accounts in the data set, but that quickly declined to 48-percent accuracy beyond the top 30,000 accounts. So, in this example, it was possible for researchers to describe the demographics and activity of a large

(20,000-user) network of active ISIL supporters with high confidence that the data set was accurate.[3]

Publics Analysis: Mapping the Argument Space in Social Media

Beyond describing the social networks of an extremist group like ISIL, the combination of SNA and lexical analysis can be used to characterize the ideological struggle over ISIL occurring on social media (Bodine-Baron, Helmus, et al., 2016).[4] This approach uses a community detection algorithm to identify the groups involved and lexical analysis to characterize those communities. This approach is a way to visualize not only who is talking to whom but also what they are talking (and care) about. The result was a social media map of the argument space around ISIL (Bodine-Baron, Helmus, et al., 2016). Figure 3.1 shows a map of the top-level metacommunities discovered in that study, along with the density and direction of connections between them.

Figure 3.1 was created using a two-step process. Community detection revealed the network structure, and lexical analysis of the content from each community characterized the groups of users—specifically, who they were demographically and what they cared about.

Detecting Communities

The first step in this approach is to collect social media data about an issue or entity of interest—in this case, more than 23 million tweets from more than 770,000 Twitter supporters and opponents of ISIL (Bodine-Baron, Helmus, et al., 2016). Domain experts suggested relevant search terms to identify likely supporters and opponents of ISIL: phrase and hashtag variants of both *Daesh* and *the Islamic Caliphate* in Arabic. The intuitive sense of domain experts could then be mechanically validated through machine reading—applying lexical analysis

---

[3] In this case, *n*-step larger analytics are possible—for example, going one additional step beyond level 1 users to examine the users they follow and then using scalable methods (e.g., machine learning) to cull the larger network from active supporters. See Berger and Morgan (2015) for more detail on this topic.

[4] The scale of this study shows why computer analytics are vital to IO efforts and to social media data collection more generally: more than 23 million tweets from 771,371 user accounts.

Figure 3.1
Pro- and Anti-ISIL Metacommunities on Twitter

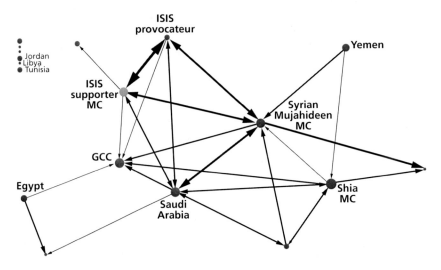

SOURCE: Bodine-Baron, Helmus, et al., 2016, p. 23, Figure 4.2; RAND analysis of Twitter data from July 2014 to May 2015.

NOTE: Thickness of the arrows indicates connections between metacommunities that are lower or higher in intensity relative to community size. Node size represents the size of the community. Red nodes indicate membership in the Sunni metacommunity. Given resource constraints, not all communities could be examined with lexical analysis; unexplored communities appear without a label. MC = metacommunity.

RAND RR1742-3.1

techniques to the collected data to see whether distinguishing between communities that used *Daesh* versus *Islamic Caliphate* accurately identified opponents and supporters, respectively (described in more detail in the next section). In this case, keyness testing showed that, indeed, the *Daesh*-using communities also used derogatory terms for ISIL (e.g., *Kharijites*, a reference to ancient opponents of mainstream Islam) and respectful terms for Arab states and Westerners (e.g., *international coalition*).[5] Communities referring to the *Caliphate* employed respectful terms for ISIL (e.g., *lions of the Islamic State*) and disrespectful terms for

---

[5]   Keyness testing involves testing the frequency of found versus expected words to detect statistically significant over- or underpresence. The expected frequencies can be measured against a general standard (e.g., a representative monolingual corpus, such as the Open

Arab states (including *apostates*) and Westerners (*crusaders*). This process served as a kind of validity measure, suggesting that these search terms were effective discriminants: The predominant use of one term over another term effectively identified a user's attitude toward ISIL.

Once a community detection algorithm has been applied to the data, this lexical validation allows an important next step. Twitter data (and data from similar platforms, such as Sina Weibo) are particularly amendable to SNA because replies, mentions, and retweets mark network interactions. By mapping out and analyzing all these interactions, a community detection algorithm can quickly group users into connected structures, but it cannot name or characterize them. The algorithm simply finds community 1, community 2, and so on. But the *Daesh*-versus-*Caliphate* discriminant immediately marked each community as pro-ISIL, anti-ISIL, or mixed in its support for the group.

Characterizing Communities

While SNA is used to analyze communities and their interactions with each other—and the *Daesh/Caliphate* discriminant showed pro- and anti- stances—from an IO perspective, the map is still blank and unlabeled. Without understanding the characteristics and concerns of the parties to the argument over ISIL, there is no plausible way to influence the conversation.

One problem is that the pool of tweets is too large for human analysis. And beyond scalability, human reliability and bias in analysis would still be an issue. Scalably and reliably characterizing these communities requires a mechanical analysis of the tweet content of the detected communities. A solution is machine-based analytic methods from corpus linguistics (lexical analysis). Lexical analysis depends on statistical tests of word frequencies or word distance, which reveal the structure of the text data. In this case, two methods were applied to the text data: *keyword* and *collocate* testing. Keywords identify statistically overpresent words in a text data set and show what the text collected is primarily about (Scott, 1996, 2001). Because keywords are weighted by

---

Source Arabic Corpus) or specific standard (e.g., a broad collection of everyday, general social media talk). For additional background on these techniques, see Scott (2001).

how statistically unusual they are, keyword testing has higher discriminant power for weaker signals. Unlike keywords, collocates are statistically conspicuous because they indicate the co-occurrence of words (Baker et al., 2008), and they often capture abstractions.[6]

Identifying Publics and Possible Influence Strategies

The automated detection of statistically significant keywords and strongly associated collocates allows the detected communities to be characterized as *publics*: abstractions of people with an advocacy stake, using shared language to address a common problem. To use an example familiar to U.S. audiences, consider an issue like gun control. On the one hand, the National Rifle Association is a real-world example of an organization involved in advocacy, but the public that uses shared language and a common goal around legitimizing private ownership of weapons is a much larger abstraction. The opposing public that seeks to limit the ownership of weapons is also larger than any formal lobbying group: It is the set of people who care about the issue, using a shared discourse to affect the debate.

Returning to our original example of discerning ISIL supporters on Twitter, SNA showed four large metacommunities, which lexical analysis could characterize as metapublics (Bodine-Baron, Helmus, et al., 2016). One community was marked by keywords and collocates reflecting Saudi concerns (including Saudi nationalism), negative secular or religious words about ISIL (terrorists, crimes and sins, excommunicates, *fitna*), and some positive words with religious connotations (praise, glory, truth, love). *A critical takeaway here is that in place of a team of analysts reading millions of tweets, a single analyst using lexical analysis software can identify a hundred or so statistically unusual words and phrases to characterize a community as a public.* The four large publics discovered in this example were as follows:

- Sunni ISIL opponents (some supporters)
- Shia ISIL opponents
- ISIL supporters

---

[6]   For example, place names ("New York City"), entities ("President Obama"), and abstract concepts ("gun control").

- Syrian mujahideen (with a mixed attitude toward ISIL).

SNA and lexical analysis together allow for an even more granular analysis, providing an empirical basis for plausible messaging to influence specific publics. Table 3.2 shows the individual publics (essentially organized around national identities and concerns) identified within the Sunni metapublic, as well as the concerns and topics of interest to each.

The topics and concerns of each public provide an empirical basis for plausible messaging strategies and targeted influence aimed at members of these publics. Here, we stress both the scalability and inductive value of this approach. This was the work of a single analyst over the course of days, not a team taking months to read hundreds of thousands of tweets. And because the analysis relies solely on user-generated social media data, there is little chance of projection—of messages that reflect U.S. cultural assumptions and priorities—and it can be done at a fairly granular level.

Table 3.2
Sunni Publics in ISIL Twitter Opposition/Support Analysis

Sunni Public	Topics and Concerns
Saudi Arabia	Threat of ISIL support and expansion in Saudi Arabia; threat to Islam posed by Iranian Shiism, secular nationalism, and the international community
Egypt	Egyptian nationalism; ISIL opposition; mistrust of the Muslim Brotherhood; frustration with U.S. policies
Jordan	Nationalism; outrage over ISIL's burning of Jordanian pilot Moath al-Kasasbeh; support for international coalition air campaign
Libya	Libyan nationalism; ISIL opposition; distrust of Libyan politicians, militants, and the West
Yemen	ISIL support; critical of Saudi Arabian intervention

SOURCE: Bodine-Baron, Helmus, et al., 2016, p. 31, Table 5.1; RAND analysis of Twitter data from July 2014 to May 2015.

Resonance Analysis: Tracking Message Diffusion over Social Media

This section details a method for tracking uptake of a group's messaging over time at a fairly granular geographic level. The proof-of-concept study described here tracked the uptake of worldview-specific language from ISIL and Muslim Brotherhood members in Egypt in 2014 (Marcellino et al., 2016). However, this method has broad potential as a measure of effectiveness, including for friendly messaging efforts.

The basis for this method is the inextricable relationship between language and worldview, where language reflects worldview, and, in turn, worldview is also shaped by language use. We can see this relationship very clearly in the language around contested issues. Consistent use of words in discourse on a particular issue does not simply reflect ideology; their use also helps circulate and spread ideology by framing issues and events in the world. Because we can model a public's discourse quantitatively, we can track uptake of a worldview as expressed through language.

Building a Linguistic Model

The first step in this method is to build a weighted linguistic model of a public's talk. In this example, it is an extremist group, but it could just as easily be a combatant command and its regional messaging. In this proof-of-concept example, analysts collected data on public talk from both ISIL and the Muslim Brotherhood (approximately 30,000 words each) and then tested the data set for both keywords and collocates. This produced a linguistic model of each group with approximately 100 statistically significant keywords and 20 two-word collocates. To help conceptualize what we mean by a *weighted linguistic model,* Table 3.3 gives some example keywords, log likelihood scores, and a translation for each word.

In this particular test, log likelihood scores over 11 are significant. In Table 3.3, double-digit scores for words like *Iraq* or *Sham* indicate that they are significantly overpresent and detectable, while scores in the hundreds (e.g., *Rafidhi*) are very strong semantic signals of what the text is primarily about. Scores over 1,000 show highly specialized talk and, thus, a characteristic signal: While words like *Safavid* may not be the top-level themes that a qualitative analyst would think of when

Table 3.3
Example ISIL and Muslim Brotherhood Keywords, Log Likelihood Ranking

ISIL			Muslim Brotherhood		
Keyword	LL	Translation	Keyword	LL	Translation
الصفوي	2,163	The Safavid	الإخوان	2,882	The Brotherhood
الدولة_الإسلامية#	643	#The Islamic State	الانقلاب	1,631	The coup
الخلافة	640	The caliphate	الشعب	914	The people
الفلوجة	427	Fallujah	الجماعة	434	The association
البيشمركة	360	The Peshmerga	المصري	395	The Egyptian
الرافضي	271	The Rafidhi	مصر	332	Egypt
الدولة	259	The state	الرئيس	329	The president
الإسلامية	585	The Islamic	الثوار	319	The revolutionaries
القاعدة	123	al Qaeda	جماعة	266	The group
العراق	78	Iraq	الانقلابيين	265	The coup supporters
الشام	62	Sham	الإرهاب	257	The terrorism

SOURCE: Marcellino et al., 2016, p. 45, Table 1.

NOTE: For log likelihood, the critical value is 10.83 (0.01%; $p < 0.001$). In this example, the minimum frequency was 20. To interpret the log likelihood (LL) scores in this table, we suggest that LL > 11 is statistically significant, between 11 and 1,000 indicates high levels of keyness (highly pointed talk), and scores above 1,000 indicate the keywords that point to extremely specialized discourses.

trying to understand ISIL's message, from an empirical perspective of trying to detect weak signals (e.g., the effects of influence), such an unexpectedly high frequency is a powerful analytic hook.

Armed with a signature—a quantitative weighted model of how these Salafist groups talk, the next step is to measure the degree of correspondence between that model and talk from the populace: Are these groups gaining or losing ground in spreading their message?

Regional Matches of Social Media Talk and Extremist Messaging

Given a linguistic model of an extremist group's talk, it is possible to see how well social media users in the general population match that talk—a quantitative match of a group's discursive market share. Imagine monitoring social media talk in the U.S. northeast on the subject of private gun ownership. Quarter-by-quarter, individuals there increased their use of such terms as *mass shootings, senseless killings,* and *innocent,* and there was less talk that included words like *responsible ownership, 2nd amendment rights,* and *criminals.* This would be strong, empirical grounds for arguing that one side was making gains in public opinion, at least in terms of framing the argument as being about the danger of guns rather than an issue of civil liberties.[7] The general process is as follows:

- *Gather social media data from a meaningful geographic population.* In our primary example, the source was Twitter data from across Egypt in 2014 geoinferenced to four regions: the Sinai, Alexandria and the coast, Upper Egypt, and Cairo and the Nile Delta. In this example, geoinferencing using both city and province names in the user location field doubled the volume of data captured, but, when back-checked against geotagged data, it had a lower confidence boundary of 80-percent accuracy.
- *Score Twitter users' feeds for statistical matches to the linguistic models.* Each user's Twitter feed can be scored by how closely it matches a linguistic model (e.g., ISIL or Muslim Brotherhood):

---

[7] We note that this approach does not allow us to answer *why* such change occurs, only observe that it happened. Causal insight would require other approaches.

- This involves summing the likelihood scores of all keywords and collocates that appear in each user's tweets and then calculating the sum expected by random chance, given the total number of words appearing in the user's tweets and the frequency/average score of keywords and collocates among all tweets.
- The resulting scores are a measure of how likely it is that matches are just random chance:
  ∘ *High* means that an account uses more than 500 percent more model (ISIL or Muslim Brotherhood) language than expected from random chance.
  ∘ *Medium* means an account uses more than 300 percent more model language than expected from random chance but less than 500 percent.
  ∘ *Low* means more than 50 percent more model language but less than 300 percent of random chance.
  ∘ *No* means that an account's language reflects random chance levels.
- *Map out change over time.* Quantified high, medium, low, and no matches at the user level can be aggregated at the regional level: a measure of the current level of diffusion of a group's messaging. Compared quarter by quarter, this is a way to both measure effectiveness over time and also, possibly, to triage other efforts.

In the example case, over the course of 2014, ISIL and the Muslim Brotherhood had low matching in the Alexandria and Cairo regions—good news from a U.S. perspective. But in both the Sinai and Upper Egypt, ISIL gained appreciably in terms of the number of high- and medium-resonance matches, while the Muslim Brotherhood lost a comparable amount. Essentially, ISIL gained market share in those two regions—bad news from a U.S. perspective. Figures 3.2 and 3.3 show this change in market share.

Stance Analysis: Detecting Messaging Strategies over Social Media
Why are some extremist messaging strategies successful while others fail? Can DoD analyze successful messaging to gain tradecraft insight

Figure 3.2
ISIL Linguistic Resonance in Egypt, 2014

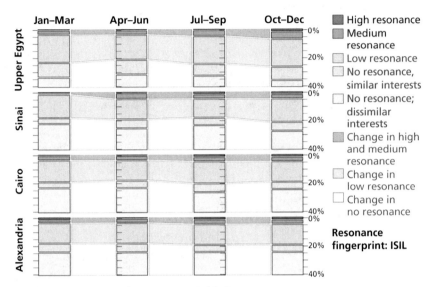

SOURCE: Marcellino et al., 2016, p. 47, Table 2.
RAND RR1742-3.2

for IO, better understand why some adversary messaging is particularly effective, and learn how to make its own messages more effective, regardless what media are used to disseminate them? Stance analysis looks at social media messaging to uncover the linguistic details of that messaging to better understand how it works. This is similar to sentiment analysis, but it is more detailed and sophisticated. Whereas the previously discussed approaches in this chapter used lexical analysis (statistical tests at the level of word counts and frequencies), this method uses statistical tests of counts and frequencies at the level of word categories. By *word categories*, we mean, for example, talk about the future or past, affect (e.g., anger, sadness, fear, positivity), certainty, values, or social relationships. Assembling categories of words into arguments is a purposeful art and reveals a detectable signal. For example, talking about the future and hope can be a strategy to motivate people, very distinct from a choice to combine talk about the past and historical wrongs. Through statistical tests on the frequency, dis-

Figure 3.3
Muslim Brotherhood Linguistic Resonance in Egypt, 2014

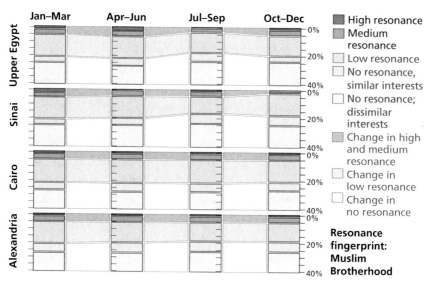

SOURCE: Marcellino et al., 2016, p. 49, Table 3.
RAND RR1742-3.3

tribution, and covariance of word categories, computer-based analysis can detect the working components of arguments and messaging at a nuts-and-bolts level (Marcellino, 2015).

As an illustration, imagine that a new chief of staff has sent a memo to uniformed and civilian members of a center. The memo is very poorly received: It was meant to inspire the staff to work together to remedy deficiencies, but instead it has the opposite effect and generates a great deal of anger at the new chief. When asked, staff might point to the "tone" of the memo—that it sounds distant and arrogant. But why, exactly, does it "sound arrogant"? Close inspection of the linguistic choices might show that the memo is rich in first- and second-person singular pronouns but entirely lacking in first-person plural pronouns: It is all "I/me" when talking solutions, "you" when talking problems, and never "us/we" in talking about anything. Even if the chief of staff did not mean this, the consistent use of pronouns in that way creates a kind of superior stance against the audience. For something like a single note, a hand-conducted analysis by a discourse analyst would be effective and efficient. However, for large volumes of social media data, computational analysis is required.

Finding Latent Factors in Social Media Talk by ISIL

To test this approach, we conducted a demonstration analysis of a collection of social media output from four extremist groups: ISIL, al-Nusrah Front, al Qaeda in the Arabian Peninsula (AQAP), and Ansar al-Sharia.[8] We used three months of translated social media output from these groups in the fourth quarter of 2014.[9] We then used state-of-the-art (as of 2015) stance analysis software to come up with word category frequencies for each corpus, which we subjected to statistical tests of frequency, distribution, and covariance to detect differences between the groups and structural regularities within each group's discourse.

For illustration, we describe in detail a single finding from this analysis: When we used exploratory factor analysis to look for latent argument structures, we found that ISIL and al-Nusrah Front had three factors (persuasive arguments, personal testimony, and a focus on shared social concerns), while AQAP's social media output had a single factor (how-to guides for technical problems). Exploratory factor analysis detects latencies through covariance in a data set by treating the correlation between a group of variables as a single, latent factor. In text analysis, this might look like future-oriented positive talk and reassuring language all covarying together: a stock "it gets better as you get older" speech. The following examples outline the factors that make AQAP's public social media talk distinct from that of al-Nusrah and ISIL.[10]

---

[8]   We note that this analysis is preliminary and was conducted as a proof of concept for the method. The data pool was relatively small (three months of social media output from the extremist groups), and the analysis used translations. While there is preliminary evidence that the software used in this analysis works well in translation (see, for example, Al-Malki et al., 2012), we strongly caveat the accuracy of the findings. Our goal in this section is to illustrate the method, not to explore particular findings from a pilot of the method.

[9]   This analysis used data from a commercial subscription to the jihadist-monitoring and analysis firm SITE Intelligence Group.

[10]   Ansar Al-Sharia had no detectable factor—that group's speech was inconsistent and lacked repeated, coherent strategies.

AQAP's Argument Strategy

AQAP's significant discriminant factor was *informational*: sharing technical and conceptual knowledge and reporting significant events.

This came out most strongly in how-to technical instructions ranging from cyberwarfare to avoiding thermal detection. For example,

> This *scene* shows a group of mujahideen trying to hide from aircraft cameras in a narrow passage, but the *thermal* recording shows their bodies clearly, <u>especially</u> <u>within this</u> low-altitude for the aircraft. Thus, it appears that the *solution* is to hide *body heat* from the aircraft cameras. <u>The way that</u> allows U.S. to do **this is** called *thermal insulation*. *Thermal insulation* **is** used in many tools that we use on a daily basis, <u>such as</u> a water thermos. It maintains the temperature of the water inside, because it contains an insulated *material* which prevents heat from escaping to the outside. *Also*, a refrigerator or what is called a freezer, and a tea thermos or what is called a container, utilize the *concept* of *insulation*.[11]

The same pattern was visible in informational reporting:

> A soldier in the turned Houthi army [member] died this *past* Thursday as a result of **his being** sniped by a mujahid from Ansar al-Shariah in Abyan province of southern Yemen. The Ansar al-Shariah News correspondent in Abyan reported that at ten in the morning this *past* Thursday, a mujahid from Ansar al-Shariah sniped a soldier in the 39th Armored Brigade <u>that is</u> stationed in the *area* of al-Mahfad of Abyan province.[12]

ISIL and Al-Nusrah Argument Strategies

Both ISIL and al-Nusrah shared three latencies. Unlike AQAP's technical approach to sharing information, ISIL and al-Nusrah used purposeful messaging strategies in the sociocultural world to persuade their audiences.

---

[11] *Concepts* are italicized, **reporting states** are bolded, and <u>specifying language</u> is underlined.

[12] *Concepts* are italicized, **reporting states** are bolded, and <u>specifying language</u> is underlined.

Outreach: Promising a Better Future

Al-Nusra (and ISIL) used similar outreach strategies. Perhaps counter-intuitively, their dominant argument strategy did not include negative or hate speech but, rather, intense, future-oriented talk that focused on positive values and relationships.[13] For example,

> Whoever <u>wants to</u> support Allah **the Great** and Almighty, then let him pledge *allegiance to* this Caliph. And whoever wants the Shariah of Allah **the Great** and Almighty to be applied, then let him pledge *allegiance to* this Caliph. Allah the Great and Almighty now distinguished the *honest* from the liar.[14]

Personal Requests and Testimony

While ISIL does not characteristically use subjective register personal "I" talk, it and al-Nusrah do use it in combination with interpersonal requests, for example in a kind of persuasive testimony:[15]

> That which **I** mention of facts **I** testify upon. **I** will underline what **my** eye saw, **my** ear heard, and **my heart** was aware of, and **I** will *tell you* what was learned second-hand. Tenth: I *ask you*, by Allah, and there is no god but He, to bring this conversation to the sheikhs and leaders in Sham [Syria] and elsewhere.[16]

A Unified Front

Another significant latency in both groups' communications was the combination of social promises and inclusive "we/our" talk. This talk is often repetitive (a hallmark of sincerity in Arabic discourse) and heavily dependent on the idea of pledging fealty or allegiance:

> In the Name of Allah, the Most Gracious, the Most Merciful The Islamic State, a blessing from Allah Abu Bakr al-Baghdadi, **we all**

---

[13] By contrast, Ansar al-Sharia and AQAP did not use this strategy.

[14] **Intensity** is bolded, *positive emotion* and *values* are italicized, and <u>future talk</u> is underlined.

[15] This strategy is missing from AQAP's social media talk.

[16] **Subjective talk** is bolded, and *addressing and requesting others* is italicized.

pledge Allegiance to him, the Amir of the State **Our** State is victorious! The Islamic State, a blessing from Allah Abu Bakr al-Baghdadi, **we all** *pledge* Allegiance to him, the Amir of the State, **Our** State, is victorious! They are fighting for victory! They force them all to kneel using mortars and PKCs [machine guns]. **Our** State is victorious! The Islamic State, a blessing from Allah Abu Bakr al-Baghdadi, **we all** *pledge* Allegiance to him, the Amir of the State **Our** State is victorious! Muslims, are you ready? After suffering for hundreds of years you will be given freedom. **Our** State is victorious![17]

Our key takeaway from this proof-of-concept analysis is that computer-based analysis of large social media data sets can provide IO tradecraft insight regarding adversary messaging. In this case, identifying outreach and argument strategies is an explanatory step that could inform countermessaging.

Automated Image Analysis: Crowdsourcing to Understand the Information Environment

This approach combines geolocation of data sources with software for image categorization and map plotting to automatically categorize and map images in very large social media data sets. Ultimately, this gives commanders the ability to see what local populations think is worth sharing (e.g., pictures of trucks, uniforms, memes, cartoons) and where they are sharing them geographically: What do people in a particular location want to share visually over social media (Bodine-Baron, Marcellino, et al., 2015)? Whereas the other approaches described in this chapter try to solve the text firehose problem—vastly more textual data than human analysts can read—this method does the same for visual data, a data type we expect will only increase in volume as mobile device penetration and network capacity increase across the globe. We think this approach has great potential for the following reasons:

- It is a low-cost form of remote data collection that does not risk other assets.

---

[17] Inclusive relationships are **bolded**, and promises are *italicized*.

- It exploits an additional data stream that should grow with increased social media penetration.
- It frees up the time and attention of expert human analysis.
- Imagery can be rich in cultural information and may be particularly valuable in areas with low literacy rates.
- It is a way of crowdsourcing what matters in the information environment: It geographically situates the imagery that local populations think is worth sharing.

We note that this is a good example of the distinction between IO and intelligence work. This method could be used as part of influence operations (What are the cultural and political concerns of the local populace?), but it could just as easily be used to collect battlefield intelligence (Where do we see more images of tanks, trucks, weapons, and uniforms being shared?). What would distinguish this as an IO effort would not be the method but, rather, the questions asked and the intent.

Step 1: Gathering Geo-Specific Social Media Data

The first step in this approach is to gather localized social media data, through either geotagging or geoinferencing.[18] Both choices have merits:

- Using only geotagged data gives both the highest confidence of accuracy of the location and the highest granularity of location. We can know confidently exactly where the social media data came from and can map that location down to the level of likely units of analysis (e.g., cities or neighborhoods). However, because the majority of social media data are not geotagged, this choice may limit the amount of available data for analysis. And because tourists tend to turn on geolocation on their mobile devices, it is possible that their images could bias the sample.

---

[18] We note that there is considerable national variation in the penetration of mobile devices, and in the volume of geotagged/inferenceable data. Thus, this approach may be more or less practical in different parts of the world.

- Geoinferencing (e.g., using both city and province names in the user location field) can capture more data at a high level of geolocation accuracy. However, it has limited granularity. In the previously mentioned example of tracking message diffusion on Egyptian social media, the 80-percent accuracy rate was only at the level of national regions.

From this set of social media data, image URLs can be stripped, and image data with location metadata can be collected, leaving a large, unsorted pile of images that a local population felt was worth sharing. The next step is to use machine tools to sort through and categorize these images.

Step 2: Automated Image Categorization

The next step is to use image categorization software on the image data set. At the time of this writing, DNNs were a promising method to break images into multiple layers of abstraction, with two caveats:

- *Processing power.* Unlike the text analytic methods discussed earlier, categorizing images is a computationally demanding task, and, to be feasible, it requires parallel computing arrays (as opposed to a single desktop system). In our example, collecting two weeks of geotagged images shared on Twitter and Facebook across Africa in 2015 resulted in 283,000 images. That required approximately three days of parallelized computing to process.
- *Categorization accuracy.* There is tension between accuracy and granularity in image categorization. At a low level of granularity (e.g., "vehicles"), current technology is highly accurate. But at higher levels of granularity (e.g., "tanks" and "trucks"), accuracy degrades.

Step 3: Plotting Images

The final step in this process is to plot these images using mapping software, to visualize what different groups are sharing. And because these data are time stamped, we can also view changes over time. As an illustration of how this might be used in support of IO, consider how images can point to and sometimes encapsulate sociocultural and political issues. In the analysis discussed in this section, the categorizer found many "comic books" that turned out to be political cartoons.[19] These and other image classes might have great value in mapping out the local information environment and showing what a populace chooses to share visually and from where they are sharing these images.

Figure 3.4 is a screenshot of the DNN tool showing automatically detected images, plotted by class (political cartoons, buildings, and vehicles) and geolocation, to form an image-sharing map.

Being able to visualize where and at what levels of density a population's concerns are being "discussed" visually could be a powerful way to understand and exploit dynamics within the information environment.

Figure 3.4
Shared Images, by Type and Geolocation

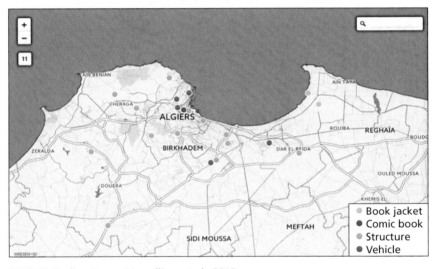

SOURCE: Bodine-Baron, Marcellino, et al., 2015.
RAND RR1742-3.4

---

[19] This highlights some current limits of image classification software. While comic books and political cartoons are very different genres to humans, they share similar visual features. Machines use different features and so have different affordances and constraints.

Context and Considerations for the Use of Social Media Analysis in Information Operations

The two previous chapters used IRCs as a framework to think about the value and insertion points for social media analysis in IO. They also presented example analytic approaches to convey the range of possibility within social media analytics and the power of creative combinations of methods. We now shift to the broader context for a DoD effort to develop social media analytical capacity. As we discuss in this chapter, existing U.S. law on data collection by DoD reflects technology from a prior era, and there is a lack of clarity on exactly what IO practitioners can and cannot do with regard to social media data. Beyond strict legal boundaries, there are also ethical issues to consider, and in a post-Snowden world in which the U.S. public is generally concerned about issues of privacy and government data collection, clarity about what constitutes legal and ethical conduct is critical to any social media analysis effort. The context for developing DoD's social media analysis capability also includes practical considerations—specifically, the cost of data collection and analysis, technology acquisition, and training.

In addressing these varied challenges to the use of social media analysis in support of IO, we recognize that they are (and are becoming more) interrelated. Our review of the relevant research draws on both the literature specific to social media use and the literature on IO writ large; much of what is applicable to IO in general is applicable to social media analysis in particular. We also draw on literature from academic research communities that are, themselves, wrestling with the problem of social media's novelty.

Legal Issues

Any consideration of the legality of building up or employing a social media analysis capability must start with the lag between *innovation* and *regulation of innovation*. DoD and civilian researchers face the same challenge:

> Because regulation of new technologies can be a slow process, assessment of all relevant legal regulations in this area of research is challenging. The lack of legal guidance specific to new technologies puts respondents potentially at risk and leaves researchers with unanswered questions. For example, consider a U.S. resident who is contacted to participate in research via social media while they are outside of the U.S. Does U.S. law apply, the law of the country the respondent is in, or the law of the country of the research organization? . . .
>
> In the absence of clear legal direction, researchers need to self-regulate . . . to accommodate the portability and flexibility of the platform on which we wish to conduct research so as to not erode the protection of human subjects. (Murphy et al., 2014, pp. 38–39)

We note a gap here between DoD and commercial perspectives on social media analytics. In our interviews with experts on commercial social media data collection and analysis, interviewees reported few concerns about collecting data in commercial contexts or in collecting data on U.S. citizens or within the United States. Concerns were focused on health-related information that is protected under the Health Insurance Portability and Accountability Act (better known as HIPAA) and any data that a company might not want to share during the discovery process for a lawsuit (interview with subject-matter expert, August 31, 2016).

While DoD faces analogous challenges with regard to social media data collection and analysis, it is not in a position to self-regulate. Rather, it must scrupulously adhere to a legal and policy framework that has not kept up with current conditions. Compliance with government contracts presents a significant problem for commercial companies because of restrictions on collecting personally identifiable information and even more stringent restrictions on data collected on U.S. citizens. This can significantly constrain the ability to collect intelligence. For example, regulations cover a wide variety of information, including an individual's Social Security number, date of birth, and fingerprints and other biometric data (DoD Directive 5400.11, 2014).

Current U.S. Law and Information Operations

Current U.S. law and policy attempt to analogically comply with international treaties that were not designed for IO and novel means of intelligence collection in support of IO, such as social media analysis (Hollis, 2009; Jurich, 2008).[1] Therefore, any attempt to implement a legally compliant social media analysis capability must account for the following.

Uncertainty About the Translation and Application of Current Law to IO

This uncertainty is a disincentive for commanders to engage in IO. Further complicating the situation, existing research on IO has tended to assume state-based warfare and ignore other factors, such as non-state actors or aggression by state-related actors below the threshold of war (e.g., ISIL propaganda and recruitment efforts, Russia's paid Internet trolls) (Duncan, 2015).

In conventional warfare with conventional weapon systems, existing law is clear in its distinction of civilian versus military targets and what constitutes legal "use of force." When engaged in conflicts outside of declared hostilities or using capabilities other than conventional

---

[1]   These international treaties include the 1868 St. Petersburg Declaration declaring "military forces" as the only legal object of war; the 1949 Geneva Conventions' Martens Clause specifying that conduct not prohibited in war is not necessarily permitted; the United Nations Charter's prohibition on the use or threat of force outside of self-defense during "armed conflict" and the principle of "civilian distinction" that prohibits military operations against civilian populations, property, and infrastructure; and Article IV of the Outer Space Treaty requiring that space be used "exclusively for peaceful purposes" (Hollis, 2009). All of these treaties were written with military kinetic use of force in mind, not military IO.

weapon systems, much of this clarity disappears. In targeting dual-use infrastructures (e.g., communication systems, social media platforms), how do commanders distinguish between combatants and noncombatants? Does countering propaganda constitute the use of force?

Finally, U.S. law regarding IO derives analogically from prohibitive law governing traditional armed conflict—focused on what cannot be done, not what can be done. This legal structure undercuts the productive potential in IO (Hollis, 2009, p. 16). In the age of instant global sharing from both traditional media (the "CNN effect") and social media, commanders have powerful reasons to shy away from using IRCs in new or different ways (Hollis, 2009).

Complexity in Overlapping Layers of Law and Policy That Might Apply to IO and IRCs

International laws on the prosecution of armed conflict (e.g., the Geneva Conventions, the United Nations Charter) are potentially applicable. IO campaigns may target or rely on space-based communication systems and platforms, and, thus, international space law may be applicable. The Constitution of the International Telecommunications Union prohibits "harmful interference" with the communication systems of other nations (while excepting military radio installations, which might or might not imply a broader range of military communication technology). Perhaps most daunting is the gap between U.S. domestic law and the domestic laws of other countries. If DoD conducts IO that, for example, includes a campaign to challenge the credibility of an extremist leader living in another country, whose law applies? Such a campaign might well include the collection and analysis of social media data. Again, complexity in legal frameworks may dissuade commanders from using IRCs to their fullest potential (Hollis, 2009).

Insufficiency in the Law Regarding IO When It Involves Nonstate Actors

State actors (e.g., Russia and China) continue to be relevant in war and IO. However, at the time of this writing, the focus in warfighting was on asymmetrical conflict with nonstate actors, such as ISIL. Information warfare is particularly appealing to nonstate actors because it is cheap, accessible, and has worldwide reach, in contrast to conventional kinetic operations. But existing domestic and international law is insufficient to address such conflicts. Beyond clear state sponsorship of an extremist group, the United States is constrained in how it may directly respond. Propaganda efforts to gain recruits or funding, for example, may not constitute armed attacks and thus may not meet U.S. self-defense thresholds (Hollis, 2009).

The uncertainty, complexity, and insufficiency of U.S. and international law regarding IO create disincentives for militaries to engage in such operations, and these factors could make a judge advocate general officer hesitant to confidently endorse the legality of a proposed IRC employment. This is an ironic and particularly frustrating problem because of IO's potential to achieve military and political objectives with less harm than conventional warfare (Hollis, 2009).

The DoD social media analysis experts whom we interviewed described U.S. law regarding the collection of publicly available information as outdated in terms of both procedure and policy, reflecting Cold War–era means and data types. They observed that DoD must conduct a legal review to remove gray areas in social media–related policy, develop clearer policies that reflect current conditions, and create service-level programs of record to put those policies into effect.

Title 10 Versus Title 50 Concerns

Title 10 and Title 50 of the U.S. Code lay out the roles and responsibilities of the U.S. military and U.S. intelligence services, respectively (Wall, 2011). The titles provide legal authority for, and distinguish between, military operations under DoD and intelligence activities and covert action by intelligence agencies. U.S. military commands that engage in IO must operate according to what is permissible under Title 10 authorities. For longer-established IRCs that might cross Title 10 and Title 50 lines (e.g., cyber), there are models under which Title 10 and Title 50 authorities are coordinated with appropriate oversight. As an example, the 24th Air Force, the Air Force component of U.S. Cyber Command, is structured to conduct operations while nimbly moving back and forth between both titles. Title 10 warfighters coordinate with the National Security Agency (NSA) to gain access to signals intelligence under NSA's Title 50 authority. The 24th Air Force also has units under Title 10 with a "U.S. Signals Intelligence Directive (USSID) that defines the limits and processes they use to collect signals intelligence under the oversight of the Air Force Intelligence, Surveillance, and Reconnaissance Agency and the authority of the NSA. These units routinely move between conducting missions under both their Title 10 and Title 50 hats" (Vautrinot, 2012).

IO planning and IRC employment involving social media and social media analytics are novel compared with established cyber activities, and there are not comparable bright-line examples. Commands that try to build a social media analysis capability may face particular scrutiny because permissible activities under Title 10 and Title 50 authorities may look very similar: Both "military and intelligence agencies possess the statutory authority to conduct intelligence-gathering activities that may be indistinguishable 'to the naked eye'" (Wall, 2011, p. 91).

So, while military commands have legal authority to conduct IO activities—activities that may seem at first glance to be clandestine under Title 50—historical and political factors have led to heightened scrutiny. One historical issue is the problem of convergence between military and intelligence operations in the post-9/11 era (Chesney, 2012). This is despite a legal architecture governing Title 10 and Title 50 operations that ideally "serves to mediate the tension between the desire for flexibility, speed, and secrecy in pursuit of national defense and foreign policy aims, on one hand, and the desire to preserve a meaningful degree of democratic accountability and adherence to the rule of law, on the other" (Chesney, 2012, p. 540). The U.S. military must prepare for changes in the operational and strategic challenges it faces, and legal architectures must also change in response.

This lag between changing operational conditions and legal architectures complicates the legitimate function of congressional oversight. While IO activities may not at first seem to fit traditional ideas of military activities, such activities as social media monitoring do not de facto trespass on Title 50:

It is Congress's antiquated oversight structure and a concomitant misunderstanding of the law that casts a shadow of concern and purported illegitimacy over military operations that resemble activities conducted by intelligence agencies. Congress's stovepiped view of national security operations is legally incongruous and operationally dangerous because it suggests statutory authorities are mutually exclusive and it creates concerns about interagency cooperation at exactly the time in history when our policy and legal structures should be encouraging increased interagency coordination and cooperation against interconnected national security threats. (Wall, 2011, p. 92)

The way to distinguish between Title 10 and 50 activities is not according to the activity per se but, rather, by the legal criteria of "command and control, as well as funding, context and mission intent" (Wall, 2011, p. 109). An example of a legitimately military activity permitted under Title 10 is a MISO effort by military units, working under a military chain of command during a humanitarian assistance/ disaster relief operation, with the intent of enhancing blue-force safety by persuading local populaces of their good intent.

Developing Clear Policy Directives on DoD's Use of Social Media Data

Given this uncertainty about the lawful use of IO across the spectrum of military operations, and given the conflicting interpretations of what constitutes Title 10 versus Title 50 activities, there is a clear need for DoD to articulate the insufficiency of current policy and law. U.S. and applicable international laws were not crafted to account for IO and novel technical means used in IO, such as social media analysis. Thus, they are applied in policy in ambiguous, analogical terms. Congress has recognized DoD's nonintelligence need to operationalize and exploit social media data and other publicly available information for a range of traditional military activities, including force protection and battlespace awareness (U.S. House of Representatives, 2016, p. 246).

This issue holds particular urgency for DoD in "that the lack of clearly defined policies is hampering [DoD's] ability . . . to understand adversarial sentiment and narrative messaging in theaters of active hostilities, as well as monitoring for non- and semi-permissive environments, and areas of potential future activity" (U.S. House of Representatives, 2016, p. 246).

As DoD develops better policy, it must of course respect U.S. ethical and legal restrictions on the collection and viewing of information on U.S. persons and address inadvertent viewing while in enemy battlespace.

Special Considerations: Collection of Information on U.S. Persons

A special challenge to the collection of social media data in support of IO is the legal prohibition on the collection of communications from U.S. persons. DoD IO activities must comply with Title 10 restrictions on domestic operations (Elstad, 2008), as well as Executive Order 12333 prohibiting the acquisition, storage, and dissemination of information on U.S. persons (see JP 3-13, 2014). The current U.S. legal framework, which is meant to safeguard privacy and restrict domestic surveillance, "did not anticipate the nature of the current threat to national security from transnational terrorism, nor did it anticipate the development of global communication networks or advanced technical methods for intelligence gathering" (Taipale, 2007, p. 130). Essentially, the existing legal framework was not written to account for the intermingling of domestic and foreign communication—which is characteristic of social media—and information collected on or about another country's populace may also include information from U.S. persons.

This raises the expectation of genuinely accidental collection of a U.S. person's information and communications while conducting foreign operations, a potentially crippling restriction on using social media data. In practical terms, compliance with a legal framework meant to prevent domestic espionage has a stifling effect on DoD operations, imposing a 90-day window on using and holding social media data, as well as third-party workarounds that potentially rob DoD analysts of critical context to find meaning in analytic results.[2]

It is not technologically feasible to completely guard against accidental collection, so a workable but legally and politically acceptable policy must be able to articulate that legitimate efforts aimed at gathering publicly available data that happen to include information on U.S. persons are not collecting data on nor focused on U.S. persons.

Ethics Issues

DoD must not only meet a legal threshold in social media analysis, but it must also meet an ethical threshold that reflects U.S. cultural values (Bartlett and Reynolds, 2015). There is thus a need to formally articulate a code of ethics for defense activities involving social media data. Particularly because of the novelty and rapid pace of innovation in social media analytics, there are bound to be courses of action that—while not explicitly forbidden by policy or law—still have the potential to violate U.S. national values.

Ethics in Internet Research Activities

The challenge in formulating an explicit code of ethics for DoD social media analysis may be informed by an analogous conversation in the civilian research community about "Internet research activity" (Markham and Buchanan, 2012). The academic research community has formal codes of ethics and monitoring and enforcement systems in place for general human research protection, but it has found that its existing ethics and rules have lagged behind advances in the field. This has resulted in a massive gap between Internet research practices and ethics practices. For example, of the 382 social media research–related articles published between 2006 and 2012, only 4 percent considered ethical issues and the implications of using Twitter as a data source (Zimmer and Proferes, 2014, p. 256). Researchers may have great free-

---

[2] For example, this could be a third-party contractor that acquires and stores social media data on behalf of DoD IO entities, presenting them with a decontextualized data layer.

dom, but there is little formal guidance on how to ethically use this new data source.

While DoD cannot simply mirror the academic world, there may be benefit in drawing from comparable work being done in the academic research community. Much like military questions around Title 10 versus Title 50, academic debates on Internet research ethics hinge on context and intent: "Conceptualizations of Internet research ethics depend on disciplinary perspectives" (Buchanan and Zimmer, 2016). And, like the military, the academic community is wrestling with the inherent complexity of social media. When planning and integrating IO, "social media" is seen as a location and means for sharing messages, a data source, and a set of analytic methods; similarly, Internet research is both a method and location for research, and it is so widely varied that it cannot be considered a single thing (Secretary's Advisory Committee on Human Resource Protections, 2013, p. 2).

The Ethics of Privacy

Beyond legal compliance, there are potential ethics-based criticisms of DoD social media analysis efforts. These criticisms may hinge on distinctions between what is considered public and what is considered private. For example, there was public criticism of the NSA's PRISM program as violating an expectation of privacy. While that case involves domestic activities that DoD will not engage in, U.S. cultural distinctions between private and public data may extend to non-U.S. data collection and operations.

Civilian research scientists face similar concerns over public and private data. The emerging position is that digital spaces can be analogically thought of as reflecting public or private real-world behavior:

> Public spaces can be likened to observing behavior in public. In situations where the terms of service clearly state that content will be made public, no consent should be necessary to conduct research on publicly available information. Researchers still need to maintain their code of ethics and protect the privacy of their research subjects. (Murphy et al., 2014, p. 6)

A common-sense approach to characterizing the public or private nature of a data source, such as Twitter, would point to the terms of service, which make clear that user input will be public. Twitter's original public API, and the public sale of Twitter data through third-party vendors, stands in contrast to social media platforms with privacy settings and user-defined networks for sharing: "[P]ublicly visible Twitter messages are guaranteed to have been published to the internet at large, at least technically, and archiving them in the course of research activities is therefore substantially less problematic" (Zimmer and Proferes, 2014, p. 13).

While we note there may be questions about how well the general public understands privacy concepts and disclosures, DoD has taken a common-sense approach, consistent with civilian researchers' positions, that treats information made broadly available as "public" (U.S. Department of Defense Manual 5240.01, 2016, p. 53).

Data and Technology Considerations

DoD must also navigate issues surrounding the acquisition of social media analytic technology and data. These issues concern not only costs but also efficacy and trade-offs among different acquisition strategies. For example, the use of commercial vendors may be attractive. Such vendors may have developed sophisticated technology in competitive marketplaces, including solutions that might be purchased off the shelf and rapidly put to use. However, there may be critical mismatches in context and purpose between commercial and military operational needs. For example, sentiment analysis for brand management is very different from sentiment analysis for insight into public argument strategies.

In our interviews with subject-matter experts in the commercial and military sectors, we found four main concerns:

- *Data and technology acquisition costs.* Data acquisition costs are rising; a good example is Twitter's decision to cut off access to data by third-party resellers and subsequent increases in data prices.

Irrespective of any cost changes, the sheer volume increase in relevant social media data, including the potential explosion of data from the Internet of Things, points to a rising tide of data acquisition costs. There are also significant costs in acquiring technology, which will be greatly affected by the acquisition strategy selected (e.g., ongoing contracting versus open-source acquisition).

- *The place of human capacity in social media analytics.* Some interviewees pointed to the scale and power of fully automated analytic systems as the most promising future. Others pointed to the need for human-based meaning and sense-making in analysis, rather than a push-button analytic approach.
- *Scaling analysis.* Experts highlighted a need for solutions to "triage" data and present human analysts with manageable streams of information. There is a need for technology that can prepare both structured and unstructured data for human sense-making.
- *Standards and sharing.* DoD requires a shared operating picture for effective social media analysis. Absent an enterprise-level solution or standard with a shared data architecture, there is no way for IO entities to share raw data, analysis results, or visualizations. Also, lacking such a standard, there is no systematic way to test new technology or methods against existing data sets.

Training Considerations

Another issue facing DoD is training. In this new domain, what skills and knowledge are needed to produce and sustain a robust and effective social media analytic capacity? DoD currently has access to both organic and contracted training across cyber specialties, including datamining. Some of this training includes elements of social media analysis, including its general applicability to IO and military operations. However, the experts we interviewed pointed out that there is a lack of training specifically meant to help analysts make meaning of social media data. As one interviewee put it, "Right now, all we can understand is 'buttonology'; push a button, get a banana" (interview with subject-matter expert, August 29, 2016). Another issue that came up was the need for oversight training in legal compliance. Given the congressional call for DoD-specific policy on the use of social media and other publicly available information, there will be a need for formal training in oversight and compliance.

CHAPTER FIVE

Recommendations

Based on our review of the literature on social media analytics in an IO context and our subject-matter expert interviews, we offer recommendations for how DoD can more efficiently and productively build up and deploy a social media analysis capability in support of IO. These recommendations cover nontechnical issues (e.g., legal and ethical concerns), doctrinal and institutional issues of implementation, and technical issues of how to usefully analyze social media data and build up technical capacity.

Develop DoD-Specific Policy and Language for Social Media Analysis

Legal Recommendations

DoD has a legitimate and pressing operational need to collect and analyze social media data. A critical challenge is that legal frameworks developed for both conventional military operations and oversight of Title 50 intelligence/covert operations have been applied to U.S. military IO. As we have detailed, these legal frameworks translate poorly, with major gaps, ambiguity, and mismatches. A necessary first step in meeting U.S. legal requirements regarding the collection and analysis of social media data—while also effectively meeting national security needs—is to articulate the meaningful difference between military information operations under Title 10 and foreign intelligence surveillance conducted under Title 50, Executive Order 12333, and the Foreign Intelligence Surveillance Act. Such an articulation should include the following:

- Make clear the relevance of command authority and intent in operations, rather than methods or source of data, in distinguishing between Title 10 and Title 50 operations. Using social media to identify a key network node for targeting with deadly force in an intelligence agency–led Title 50 operation is categorically different from using the same method and data to identify a network node in support of a MISO effort.
- Distinguish between "use of force" in conventional operations and the use of nonkinetic IRCs, such as MISO or public affairs. Current law reflects U.S. values by distinguishing between combatants and noncombatants in the use of force, but it stumbles if it mischaracterizes, for example, counterpropaganda efforts that are intended to reduce conflict as a "use of force."
- Address the complexity of overlapping layers of domestic law and policy that might apply to IO and IRCs, as well how to address differences between U.S. and other nations' applicable laws.
- Inform policy and doctrine with clear principles meant to reasonably protect U.S. persons from data collection, and distinguish between operations directed at domestic persons and operations that may inadvertently collect data on U.S. persons as a by-product of the global reach of modern communication systems and social media.

Develop Title 10–Specific Language for Social Media Analysis

DoD has been using the language and conceptual framework of Title 50 entities, and the use of words such as *collection* and *retention* reinforces an intelligence/covert framework, as opposed to a military operations/IO one. In developing policy that reflects its needs, DoD should establish precise, distinct terms of art for social media data acquisition, storage, and analysis, and it should insert that language into doctrine and policy memoranda. Examples might include eliminating the term *collection* in favor of *acquisition*, or *retention* in favor of *storage*.

Ethical Recommendations

In addition to ensuring legal compliance in IO, a plausible and sustainable social media capability that meets national security needs must also account for ethical standards in U.S. culture. Our recommendations for ethics considerations include process choices, suggested best practices, and specific recommendations regarding privacy controls.

Principles Versus Codes

As an overarching process recommendation, we think DoD should formulate and publish flexible *principles of conduct* rather than sets of hard-and-fast rules. This is particularly important given the rapidly evolving nature of social media technologies and trends. This will also allow U.S. military commanders to operationalize ethical conduct in locally contextualized ways, inductively producing ethical outcomes to a greater extent than would be possible under codified rule sets (Markham and Buchanan, 2012, p. 5).

Data Collection Best Practices

DoD should develop a set of standards-based best practices for the collection of social media data that reflect U.S. values and do not impede mission accomplishment. A workable set of practices should include the following elements (Bartlett and Reynolds, 2015):

- When possible, make research aims and methods public and explicit while protecting tradecraft and ongoing operations.
- Establish a well-developed and explicit principle of "proportionality" that balances collection intrusiveness against reasonable national security needs.
- Take reasonable safeguards to ensure that methods for storage and distribution of social media data sets—even anonymized ones—protect persons from being identified through cross-referencing or triangulation.
- Develop and publish standards for weighing the risk that collection efforts pose to the free and open use of social media and the Internet against national security benefits. Such a standard should also include an assessment of the justification for using public funds for a given collection effort.

- Develop and publish a standard on the reasonable expectation of privacy for DoD collection of social media data that balances national security needs and public expectations of transparency (Bartlett and Reynolds, 2015).

Recommendations for Implementation and Integration

Our analysis addressed *how* social media analysis could be integrated effectively into DoD IO, as well as *ways* of implementing these approaches. We offer the following recommendations concerning DoD's implementation of a social media analytic strategy.[1]

An IRC-Based Framework for Implementation

Big data approaches to IO, including social media analysis, are in their nascent stage. The newness of social media concepts, vocabulary, and practices presents a barrier to adoption and implementation. Linking new information with known information will help DoD better incorporate these new methods and tools. Chapter Two presented an initial IRC-based framework for understanding and implementing social media analysis as a starting point for its insertion into IO doctrine and practice.

An Enterprise-Level Social Media Analysis Effort

Current efforts to build a social media analysis capability within DoD are local and uncoordinated across and between echelons. Social media analytic approaches are being used to solve problems at combatant commands and within the services at the command level. This distributed set of efforts may lead to innovation by providing many incubation sites, but a lack of unity has multiple drawbacks:

---

[1]   DoD should carefully consider how best to build capacity from a personnel management perspective. This report does not make specific recommendations about the advantages and disadvantages of developing capacity by training members versus hiring government employees or using contractors, but the issue still stands and should be addressed.

- It precludes the possibility of cost savings through an enterprise-level effort. This is particularly important in terms of data acquisition costs, but there may also be cost savings for both technology acquisition and training from a coordinated DoD-wide effort.
- It increases the risk of stovepipes.

Therefore, we recommend that DoD consider the benefits and risks of an enterprise-level social media analysis effort.

Technical Recommendations

Technology Acquisition

Our review of social media analytic approaches favors existing, open-source technologies and methods. While we acknowledge that solutions from the commercial sector may be technologically sophisticated and have great potential, there are also possible drawbacks in terms of the cost and applicability of transferring such solutions. To move forward with social media analysis, DoD must weigh the costs and benefits of using open-source versus commercial solutions. In particular, it should consider the following trade-offs:

- Commercial vendors have a vested interest in keeping advances secret and proprietary, so they tend to produce "black-box" solutions that show only results (not processes) to users. Black-box solutions may be quite sophisticated, but unless someone in the enterprise can look under the hood and see the process, including built-in assumptions, trade-offs, and proxy decisions, the validity of the results cannot be confirmed.
- Commercial entities' monetization strategies may work against the government's interest. For example, negotiating an ongoing contract to provide services may be an inefficient use of public funds when compared with a "teach-me-to-fish" approach that puts usable tools and workflows in the hands of DoD analysts.
- Not all technologies or solutions translate to DoD operational contexts and realities.

Training and Skill Acquisition

Current training in cyber specialties within DoD is insufficient to support a robust social media analysis capability. To address this shortfall, we offer the following recommendations:

- Given congressional calls for specific policy on the use of social media and other publicly available information, there will be a need for formal training within DoD on oversight and compliance.
- To the degree that DoD chooses to build a social media analysis capacity using military personnel, training should go beyond "buttonology" to teach analysts how to make meaning of social media data.

Table 5.1 provides a summary of next steps for DoD as it continues to explore the factors involved in developing and implementing a social media analysis capability and as it addresses the legal and policy challenges to doing so.

Table 5.1
Roadmap for Leveraging Social Media Analysis for DoD IO Campaigns

Action	Outcome
Conduct DoD-level legal review of support for IO by Title 10 organizations.	Update to JP 3-13, Information Operations, that presents clear legal guidance and limitations for commanders and IO planners, including Title 10–specific language for IO-centric data use
Formulate clear guidelines for IO-centric data acquisition, storage, and use within DoD. These guidelines should be informed by similar efforts from academic and industry leaders.	DoD policy memorandum that makes policy guidelines explicit and sets standards for weighing the risks and benefits to national security
Analyze the strengths and weaknesses of DoD's enterprise-level social media analysis capacity, opportunities and costs of its development (including training), and the characteristics of the threats it faces.	Explicit policy decision between either current ad hoc service/combatant command social media analytic efforts or an enterprise-level effort across DoD
Commission an independent review to advise the U.S. government on technology acquisition, focusing on the benefits and trade-offs of open-source versus commercial acquisition strategies.	DoD policy memorandum that outlines criteria for commercial technology acquisition in support of social media analysis

References

Abbasi, Mohammad-Ali, Shamanth Kumar, Jose Augusto Andrade Filho, and Huan Liu, "Lessons Learned in Using Social Media for Disaster Relief—ASU Crisis Response Game," *Lecture Notes in Computer Science*, Vol. 7227, New York: Springer, 2012, pp. 282–289.

Al-Malki, Amal, David Kaufer, Suguru Ishizaki, and Kira Dreher, *Arab Women in Arab News: Old Stereotypes and New Media*, London: Bloomsbury, 2012.

Baker, Paul, Costas Gabrielatos, Majid Khosravinik, Michał Krzyżanowski, Tony McEnery, and Ruth Wodak, "A Useful Methodological Synergy? Combining Critical Discourse Analysis and Corpus Linguistics to Examine Discourses of Refugees and Asylum Seekers in the UK Press," *Discourse and Society*, Vol. 19, No. 3, May 2008, pp. 273–306.

Bartlett, Jamie, and Louis Reynolds, *The State of the Art 2015: A Literature Review of Social Media Intelligence Capabilities for Counter-Terrorism*, London: Demos, 2015.

Berger, J. M., and Jonathon Morgan, *The ISIS Twitter Census: Defining and Describing the Population of ISIS Supporters on Twitter*, Washington, D.C.: Brookings Institution, March 2015. As of March 16, 2017: https://www.brookings.edu/research/the-isis-twitter-census-defining-and-describing-the-population-of-isis-supporters-on-twitter

Bodine-Baron, Elizabeth, Todd C. Helmus, Madeline Magnuson, and Zev Winkelman, *Examining ISIS Support and Opposition Networks on Twitter*, Santa Monica, Calif.: RAND Corporation, RR-1328-RC, 2016. As of March 16, 2017: http://www.rand.org/pubs/research_reports/RR1328.html

Bodine-Baron, Elizabeth, William Marcellino, Doug Yeung, and Zev Winkelman, "Social Media Analysis Across Language and Geography," presentation at the conference Social Media and Online Behavior: Language and Culture Considerations and Challenges for the Intelligence Community, College Park, Md., June 11, 2015.

Boehnert, John M., *Influencing Tomorrow: A Study of Emerging Influence Techniques and Their Relevance to United States Information Operations*, thesis, Fort Leavenworth, Kan.: U.S. Army Command and General Staff College, 2015.

Buchanan, Elizabeth A., and Michael Zimmer, "Internet Ethics Research," *Stanford Encyclopedia of Philosophy*, revised August 24, 2016. As of March 16, 2017:
https://plato.stanford.edu/entries/ethics-internet-research/

Chesney, Robert, "Military-Intelligence Convergence and the Law of the Title 10/Title 50 Debate," *Journal of National Security Law and Policy*, Vol. 5, No. 2, 2012, pp. 539–629.

Correa, Denzil, and Ashish Sureka, "Solutions to Detect and Analyze Online Radicalization: A Survey," *IITD PhD Comprehensive Report*, Vol. 5, No. N, January 2013. As of March 16, 2017:
https://arxiv.org/pdf/1301.4916v1.pdf

Dauber, Cori E., *YouTube War: Fighting in a World of Cameras on Every Cell Phone and Photoshop on Every Computer*, Carlisle Barracks, Pa.: Strategic Studies Institute, U.S. Army War College, November 2009. As of March 16, 2017:
http://www.au.af.mil/au/awc/awcgate/ssi/youtubewar_dauber.pdf

DoD—*See* U.S. Department of Defense.

Drapeau, Mark, and Linton Wells II, *Social Software and National Security: An Initial Net Assessment*, Monterey, Calif.: Center for Technology and National Security Policy, National Defense University, April 2009.

Duncan, Matthew, *Future Casting Influence Capability in Online Social Networks*, Toronto, Ont.: Defence Research and Development Canada, 2015.

Elstad, Peter L., *Overcoming Information Operations Legal Limitations in Support of Domestic Operations*, thesis, Fort Leavenworth, Kan.: U.S. Army Command and Staff College, 2008.

Everstine, Brian, "Carlisle: Air Force Intel Uses ISIS 'Moron's' Social Media Posts to Target Airstrikes," *Air Force Times*, June 4, 2015. As of March 16, 2017:
http://www.airforcetimes.com/story/military/tech/2015/06/04/air-force-isis-social-media-target/28473723

Gendron, Jr., Gerald R., Herminio Blas-Irizarry, and Jesse W. Boggs, *Next-Generation Strategic Communication: Building Influence Through Online Social Networking*, thesis, Norfolk, Va.: Joint and Combined Warfighting School, Joint Forces Staff College, June 2009.

Gilinsky, Jaron, "How Social Media War Was Waged in Gaza-Israel Conflict," MediaShift, February 13, 2009. As of March 16, 2017:
http://mediashift.org/2009/02/how-social-media-war-was-waged-in-gaza-israel-conflict044

Goolsby, Rebecca, *On Cybersecurity, Crowdsourcing, and Social Cyber-Attack*, Washington, D.C.: Wilson Center, 2013. As of March 16, 2017: https://www.wilsoncenter.org/sites/default/files/127219170-On-Cybersecurity-Crowdsourcing-Cyber-Attack-Commons-Lab-Policy-Memo-Series-Vol-1.pdf

Hollis, Duncan B., "New Tools, New Rules: International Law and Information Operations," in G. J. David, Jr., and T. R. McKeldin, eds., *Ideas as Weapons: Influence and Perception in Modern Warfare*, Washington, D.C.: Potomac Books, 2009, pp. 59–72.

Joint Publication 3-13, *Information Operations*, Washington, D.C.: U.S. Joint Chiefs of Staff, incorporating change 1, November 20, 2014.

JP—*See* Joint Publication.

Jurich, Jon P., "Cyberwar and Customary International Law: The Potential of a Bottom-Up Approach to an International Law of Information Operations," *Chicago Journal of International Law*, Vol. 9, No. 1, Summer 2008, pp. 275–295.

Kase, Sue E., Elizabeth K. Bowman, Tanvir Al Amin, and Tarek Abdelzaher, *Exploiting Social Media for Army Operations: Syrian Civil War Use Case*, Aberdeen Proving Ground, Md.: Army Research Laboratory, July 2014.

Katz, Yaakov, "Facebook Details Cancel IDF Raid," *Jerusalem Post*, March 4, 2010. As of March 16, 2017: http://www.jpost.com/Home/Article.aspx?id=170156

Keller, Rebecca A., *Influence Operations and the Internet: A 21st Century Issue*, Maxwell Air Force Base, Ala.: Air War College, Air University, Paper No. 52, February 17, 2010. As of March 16, 2017: http://www.au.af.mil/au/awc/awcgate/maxwell/mp52.pdf

Khazan, Olga, "Russia's Online-Comment Propaganda Army," *The Atlantic*, October 9, 2013. As of March 16, 2017: http://www.theatlantic.com/international/archive/2013/10/russias-online-comment-propaganda-army/280432

Kumar, Shamanth, Geoffrey Barbier, Mohammad Ali Abbasi, and Huan Liu, "TweetTracker: An Analysis Tool for Humanitarian and Disaster Relief," *Proceedings of the Fifth International AAAI Conference on Weblogs and Social Media*, Palo Alto, Calif.: Association for the Advancement of Artificial Intelligence, 2011, pp. 661–662.

Laje, Diego, "#Pirate? Tracking Modern Buccaneers Through Twitter," CNN, March 15, 2012. As of March 16, 2017: http://www.cnn.com/2012/03/15/business/somalia-piracy-twitter

Levin, Megan, "Social Media and Intelligence," presentation, Embry-Riddle Aeronautical University, Prescott, Ariz., Spring 2015. As of March 16, 2017: http://commons.erau.edu/pr-honors-csi/1/?utm_source=commons.erau.edu%2Fpr-honors-csi%2F1&utm_medium=PDF&utm_campaign=PDFCoverPages

Marcellino, William M., "Revisioning Strategic Communication Through Rhetoric and Discourse Analysis," *Joint Force Quarterly*, No. 76, First Quarter 2015, pp. 52–57. As of March 16, 2017:
http://ndupress.ndu.edu/Media/News/News-Article-View/Article/577589/jfq-76-revisioning-strategic-communication-through-rhetoric-and-discourse-analy

Marcellino, William M., Kim Cragin, Joshua Mendelsohn, Andrew Cady, Madeline Magnuson, and Kathleen Reedy, "Measuring the Popular Resonance of Daesh's Propaganda," *Journal of Strategic Security*, Vol. 10, No. 1, 2016, pp. 32–52.

Markham, Annete, and Elizabeth Buchanan, *Ethical Decision-Making and Internet Research: Recommendations from the AoIR Ethics Working Committee (Version 2.0)*, Chicago, Ill.: Association of Internet Researchers, 2012. As of March 16, 2017:
https://aoir.org/reports/ethics2.pdf

Murphy, Joe, Michael W. Link, Jennifer Hunter Childs, Casey Langer Tesfaye, Elizabeth Dean, Michael Stern, Josh Pasek, Jon Cohen, Mario Callegaro, and Paul Harwood, *Social Media in Public Opinion Research: Report of the AAPOR Task Force on Emerging Technologies in Public Opinion Research*, Oakbrook Terrace, Ill.: American Association for Public Opinion Research, 2014. As of March 16, 2017:
https://www.aapor.org/AAPOR_Main/media/MainSiteFiles/AAPOR_Social_Media_Report_FNL.pdf

Nelson, Anne, "How Mapping, SMS Platforms Saved Lives in Haiti Earthquake," MediaShift, January 11, 2011. As of March 16, 2017:
http://mediashift.org/2011/01/how-mapping-sms-platforms-saved-lives-in-haiti-earthquake011

Omand, David, Jamie Bartlett, and Carl Miller, "Introducing Social Media Intelligence (SOCMINT)," *Intelligence and National Security*, Vol. 27, No. 6, 2012, pp. 801–823.

Opperman, Duane A., *Information Operations and Public Affairs: A Union of Influence*, Carlisle Barracks, Pa.: U.S. Army War College, March 2012.

Oreskovic, Alexei, "Here's Another Area Where Twitter Appears to Have Stalled: Tweets per Day," *Business Insider*, June 15, 2015. As of March 16, 2017:
http://www.businessinsider.com/twitter-tweets-per-day-appears-to-have-stalled-2015-6

Phillips, Kenneth N., and Aaron Pickett, "Embedded with Facebook: DoD Faces Risks from Social Media," *Crosstalk Magazine*, May–June 2011, pp. 25–29.

Schoen, Rudy, *Social Media: Valuable Tools in Today's Operational Environment*, Newport, R.I.: Joint Military Operations Department, 2011.

Scott, Mike, Wordsmith Tools, software, version 7.0, Lexical Analysis Software and Oxford University Press, 2016.

———, "Mapping Key Words to Problem and Solution," in Mike Scott and Geoff Thompson, eds., *Patterns of Text: In Honour of Michael Hoey*, Amsterdam, The Netherlands: John Benjamins Publishing Co., 2001, pp. 109–128.

Secretary's Advisory Committee on Human Research Protections, "Considerations and Recommendations Concerning Internet Research and Human Subjects Research Regulations, with Revisions," Rockville, Md.: Office for Human Research Protections, U.S. Department of Health and Human Services, March 13, 2013. As of March 16, 2017:
https://www.hhs.gov/ohrp/sites/default/files/ohrp/sachrp/mtgings/2013%20March%20Mtg/internet_research.pdf

Spencer, Robert, "Stage-Managed Massacre," *FrontPageMag*, August 2, 2006. As of March 16, 2017:
http://archive.frontpagemag.com/readArticle.aspx?ARTID=3281

Taipale, K. A., "The Ear of Dionysus: Rethinking Foreign Intelligence Surveillance," *Yale Journal of Law and Technology*, Vol. 9, Spring 2007, pp. 128–161.

U.S. Department of Defense Directive 5400.11, *DoD Privacy Program*, October 29, 2014.

U.S. Department of Defense Manual 5240.01, *Procedures Governing the Conduct of DoD Intelligence Activities*, August 8, 2016.

U.S. House of Representatives, Committee on Armed Services, report on H.R. 4909, National Defense Authorization Act for Fiscal Year 2017, with additional views, Washington, D.C., May 4, 2016. As of March 16, 2017:
https://www.congress.gov/114/crpt/hrpt537/CRPT-114hrpt537.pdf

Vautrinot, Suzanne M., "Sharing the Cyber Journey," *Strategic Studies Quarterly*, Vol. 6, No. 3, Fall 2012, pp. 71–87.

Wall, Andru E., "Demystifying the Title 10–Title 50 Debate: Distinguishing Military Operations, Intelligence Activities and Covert Action," *Harvard National Security Journal*, Vol. 3, 2011, pp. 85–141.

Watts, Duncan J., and Peter Sheridan Dodds, "Influentials, Networks, and Public Opinion Formation," *Journal of Consumer Research*, Vol. 34, No. 4, December 2007, pp. 441–458.

Xiong, Fei, and Yun Liu, "Opinion Formation on Social Media: An Empirical Approach," *Chaos*, Vol. 24, No. 1, March 2014.

Zeitzoff, Thomas, "Does Social Media Influence Conflict? Evidence from the 2012 Gaza Conflict," *Journal of Conflict Resolution*, June 7, 2016.

Zeitzoff, Thomas, John Kelly, and Gilad Lotan, "Using Social Media to Measure Foreign Policy Dynamics: An Empirical Analysis of the Iranian-Israeli Confrontation (2012–13)," *Journal of Peace Research*, Vol. 52, No. 3, May 2015, pp. 368–383.

Zimmer, Michael, and Nicholas John Proferes, "A Topology of Twitter Research: Disciplines, Methods, and Ethics," *Aslib Journal of Information Management*, Vol. 66, No. 3, 2014, pp. 250–261.